SOME OF THE LIGHT

ALSO BY THE AUTHOR

NONFICTION
All They Will Call You

FICTION
Mañana Means Heaven
Breathing, In Dust

POETRY
Natural Takeover of Small Things
Culture of Flow
Skin Tax
The Central Chakrah Project (CD)

SOME
OF THE
LIGHT

New and Selected Poems

TIM Z. HERNANDEZ

Raised Voices / BEACON PRESS / Boston

Beacon Press
Boston, Massachusetts
www.beacon.org

Beacon Press books are published under the auspices of
the Unitarian Universalist Association of Congregations.

25 24 23 22   8 7 6 5 4 3 2 1

This book is printed on acid-free paper that meets the
uncoated paper ANSI/NISO specifications for permanence
as revised in 1992.

Text design by Kevin Barrett Kane
at Wilsted & Taylor Publishing Services

Raised Voices: A poetry series established in 2021 to raise
marginalized voices and perspectives, to publish poems
that affirm progressive values and are accessible to a wide
readership, and to celebrate poetry's ability to access truth
in a way that no other form can.

Library of Congress Cataloging-in-Publication Data
is available for this title.
Paperback: 978-0-8070-0669-6
e-book: 978-0-8070-0670-2

For RUMI and SALVADOR—

when it was just us.

In your beautiful world, says
In your fresh world, says
In your world of clarity, says
You are a green Father, says
A Father of clarity, says
Your words are medicine, says
Your breath is medicine . . .

—Maria Sabina, Mazatec healer

CONTENTS

SOME OF THE LIGHT

Endling   4

Refraction #1   7

Father of Clarity   9

A Basic Understanding   12

Refraction #2   15

Single Parent Soliloquy (& The Joy of Kites)   16

This City   20

Refraction #3   22

Self Portrait at 46   24

Time Capsule   26

Limerence   29

Unqualified Poem   31

Refraction #4   38

Settling   39

Sandalwood   42

Salvador   44

The Poet's Return   47

Refraction #5   48

Hometown Ode   50

Ish   52

Tik Tok   55

Brown Lotus (A Performance)   57

Her Majesty's Last Stand   63

Variations on *This Land*   69

Refraction #6   72

Sleepless Nights (Thich Nhat Hanh Is Dying)   73

A Grocery Store   81
The Talk (Talisman for Salvador)   83

NATURAL TAKEOVER OF SMALL THINGS
Home   91
Brown Christ   92
The Day Johnny Tapia Died on My Sidewalk   93
Undelivered Postcards to Lydia   94
San Joaquin Sutra   97
Natural Takeover of Small Things   108
Instructions for the Altar   109
Flying Parallel   113
My Name Is Hernandez   114
Adios, Fresno   118

CULTURE OF FLOW
Culture of Flow   125
How to Get to the San Joaquin River   139

SKIN TAX
Mama's Boy   145
I Rub My Hands   149
I Arrive Late   153
I Pissed on Little Ricky   155
Perched on the Face   156
If I Could Tell You   158
Enter Madrugada   160
I'm Going to Put Virgil Down   162
When Young Andres   165

Acknowledgments   167
Publication Acknowledgments   169
About the Author   171

SOME OF THE LIGHT

True contemplation *is* resistance.

—Ernesto Cardenal

4.27.20

Today, I witnessed—
a parade of leaves marching
down Stanton Street, in groups of ten,
maybe more, taunting us with their natural freedom.
Outside, the Palo Verde tree trembles
in the oncoming heat, while the windows
gossip with the blown particles
of a glass I broke. Each refraction,
a glimpse of our despair. The rumor goes—
inside this house lives an aging man,
head of raven and ice, with two children,
and everything to lose.
These days have turned futile.
We can't live this way much longer.
We are the stars, and we are the darkness
that surrounds the stars. And we are the ether
and the emptiness, and the desirous
distance between the two.

I must remember this.

ENDLING

For Ana Saldaña

I once drove to meet a hummingbird
at the foot of the Canadian border.
And I would do it again.
I'm such a willing flower.
Lean into a sun that shines on me.
I'm bending now, toward you.
I promised myself I'd abstain
from toxic plants. I want to turn to palm readers,
but the moment I catch myself opening
that neon door, I worry
where their hands have been.
In places of worship, I find myself
longing to be rescued. Say, a botanical garden.
Or White Sands, N.M. Or on the top step
of my porch overlooking Ciudad Juárez.
I can't help it. She took me by the hand
once to Chief Joseph's grave, and we made
shadow-prayers out of bare wings.
She said, *All he wanted was to go home.*
I left a note pinned to a tree:
I was here. You were not. Can you
forgive us for this mess we've made?
It's been five years and three months
without a drink. The longest
my liver has ever gone
without turning sentimental.
Nothing gets away from me anymore.

What I'm getting at here is that I've spent
this year walking back
the sum of my hangovers.
Starting with you.
Starting with that electricity line
that caught me one wintery night.
Starting with that liquor store curb in Albuquerque,
and onto that snaking Red River in the San Luis Valley.
I found the rest stop outside Denver that held us,
and I unsmoked all the cigarettes,
rolled the planes back over
the Rockies, and returned the watercolors
to Nature Boy's pond in western Mass.
Never before had so many stones
been upturned in Marfa, Texas, nor
have all the Ferris wheels wound
backwards so fast. Do you know
how many pressed white bed sheets
it takes to undo the shadows?
I've been moon-walking across your memory,
restoring sunsets to their rightful coast.
Last night, someone held up a sign on the nightly
news, it said: *Welcome to the End.*
But it just kept on, until
the sign carrier eventually grew tired,
and walked home.
All he wanted was to go home,
I could hear her saying.
There are more affectionate ways
to measure these days with than masturbation.
Yesterday, a murmuration of birds composed a poem
in the sky. It read: *Jack Collom is dead*
So the magpies along the Front Range

have taken to yodeling honorific elegies,
and I can almost hear Jack cry out,
They're crazier than poets!
Everything is black or white with them!
They tell me California is on fire,
and old things are burning up.
History is going to dregs.
And there is still a wolf in the hen house.
Everyone is saying something
to no one listening. Everyone wants
to wade in a gutter and call themselves
a prophet without first learning
how to kneel.

REFRACTION #1

The Children

go with their mother for a visit.
We can only ever return to our mothers for a visit.
But we can never again be the child who once visited.
We share physical space, but the head remains.
Nostalgic of what we can't have.
Enamored with what we thought we knew.
& the heart's obsession with time travel.
Geography and guilt, both made of matter.
The girl, the boy, the mother—a nursery rhyme:
Note the wording in this note.
Not the wording in the knot.
Heal the herding of the heart.
Halt the timing of the clock.
Rewrite the beginning we simply cannot.

5.12.20

I refuse to leave my home.
I must write this down. Behind masks
they are protesting, coast to ghost,
another George Floyd extinguished
by a dull shield, and another mother unravels,
her dignity before the cameras.
We are passive voyeurs of our own parade.
We invest in material. In matter. Not lives.
Black or otherwise. Nothing matters.
Of matter we are made. Of matter
we disintegrate. We get madder. Get numb.
Lust words like, justice, *nurse rhetorical*
hangovers by morning. But we've had
our hearts broken before,
and we've put them back together ourselves.
We have chosen not to remember things.
For the sake of our own progress.
Everyone is on trial. No longer are we afforded
to look away. The hospitals have closed,
and medicine must be administered at home now.
We must heal ourselves.

Remember this.

FATHER OF CLARITY

Each day the same now,
I wake her up—she's a woman
in the making, and me,
I'm still a boy, given this responsibility
of another, and my boy,
he's visiting his mother, one
thousand miles away. We drive
to school each morning, discussing
the state of all things—
how she will need to use my razor
blades, *for my legs*, she says,
and armpits, except she doesn't say
armpits, she says, *for under my arms*.
I mention the color of the sky
at 8:15 a.m. being something like
the color of her eyes seconds after she was born.
She responds by asking me
what "verisimilitude" means, and I tell her
to look it up. These are
the particulars of raising Rumi.
Not like when we would once hold hands
and write our names in the snow.
Not like when she would fall asleep
in the bicycle seat tethered to my back,
as we rode down Colorado pathways.
This is El Paso, the face without

makeup. We cannot hide behind
hiding any longer.
The dry cycle never dries the first
go-round. Living alone is learning
to speak for both sides
of the conversation. And God,
isn't this true? And God replies,
it is only verisimilitude.
Lately, I don't have
much to say, except I wish
I could go back to *Hejira* and
that rainy café in Asheville, North Carolina.
I wish I could go back to the back
of the beginning, try again. Like a video game,
hit the reset button, throw
a love tantrum, force round pegs to fit
my square anatomy. I've always wanted
a kitchen with a view of both sides,
and now I've got two, El Paso / Juárez.
It's like looking through a kaleidoscope that refracts
the surreality of our days. See here,
a mountain preaches, with accent:
La Biblia es la verdad, leéla.
See here, the river howls in American twang:
Go back to where you come from.
Between the two, a chaparral bows:
This is not what brotherhood looks like.
This is not the conversation for Rumi though.
She reminds me of this. Held up the bird.
Unnamed still. Trained it to land on her finger.
How it returns to its cage when it flies
too far. I'm the opposite. I return to flying
when I'm too far in the cage.

She's always been a friend-soul
to me. More than a daughter.
The hierarchy is this: I make her
eggs with arugula and toast. She eats them.
We attempt yoga in the mornings.
There is a peacefulness in our routine.
We don't speak about the day
when all of this
will be nothing more
than a poem.

A BASIC UNDERSTANDING

If you are human, staring
out two eyes, speaking out
two lips, breathe two lungs,
moves one tongue—
then you will see clearly
that your entire life, all the needs,
the sustenance, condiments, basic
breath you breathe, the joy
you chase, to play a very basic
role in your children's lives, cello lessons,
baseball games, chore charts
—to say to oneself, I am basically
productive at what I do, and kiss
your beloved at the ripe peak of her
parted lips, and then find yourself
sitting to a plate of toast, butter, coffee
with cream and sugar, a basic meal,
perhaps less indulgent than the night before—
then you will see clearly that your own hopes
are tethered to one kitchen, or another,
and all kitchens lead through a cloud, a basic
harvest of wind and particle, all kitchens
lead through rain, lead through one vast field
or another, no meal exempt from this basic
journey, all meals lead through dirt, lead
through sediment and root, through bark
and stem and vine, lead through basic sun
no machinations necessary, all meals

lead through blossom and burst—
a legume, a nut, a basic green leaf, elephant heart
plum, a tuber, tomato, sprig, grove of citrus,
and in that grove, or end of every vine, basic
to the journey, rising there, amid fragrant clusters,
are two hands, four hands, a thousand
basically dirty, calloused hands, culling
the gems from ones gone to rot—
and the diesels will transport, fuel to roll the wheels,
rubber from the Amazon, all kitchens lead through
rubber, all rubber leads through rain,
rain leads through us, no one denied—
if you are human, staring out
two eyes, speaking out
two lips, breathe two lungs,
moves one tongue—
Then you will see clearly that the cloud,
the air, particles, pollutants, condiments,
the hope, the kids, the kiss, the cello,
chores, the sugar, the field, the kitchen,
the elephant, plums, the fragrance, the gem,
the dirt, two basic hands, the Amazon,
and the rains, and the kitchen
you've been lead through,
are all basically your journey too.

6.9.20

Rumi sang Both Sides Now
nonstop tonight. The trains over Ciudad Juárez
sang from both sides now, nonstop tonight.
I reached my virtual limit tonight. I resorted
to moments gone, and begged to be held
once and for goddamn all tonight.
I threatened to scale all the walls tonight.
But I couldn't convince the unmarked helicopters
to seize me. No one can. Has it always been
this long out of control? Help is not on the way.

We must remember this.

REFRACTION #2

A Man

goes before the judge
to make the case for Fatherhood.
The courtroom is stymied by the apparition.
Rosaries are clutched, prayers whispered.
Even the judge, in her cloak of indecision, leans back.
The mother is there, pushing against silence.
A thousand stories are exchanged.
From the disembodied mouths of the children.
In these halls the word *love* echoes like a myth.
As if years ago, in some distant land,
existed two birds, who tried forging themselves into one,
but wound up resentful
at the impermanent nature of flight.
Right now, the parents of 14,000 children in cages
still believe in such miracles.

SINGLE PARENT SOLILOQUY (& THE JOY OF KITES)

Who has time for poetry anymore?
I'm writing this as I'm walking.
There is muzak on the loudspeakers
of the dentist's office, and I must
make poetry of it, if I am to make
anything at all anymore. Somewhere outside,
in San Jacinto Plaza, teachers have gathered
to protest, they want to occupy.
Somewhere here there is always a protest.
And it's usually happening
when I am occupied. So, I've decided
to protest on my own. I declare out loud, to no one,
I will make the appointment for this pain in my gut!
But I will fail at making the appointment.
I am boycotting this house!
My mother used to say this, and now I see why.
Some days I catch myself writing
simply to remind myself, I am a poet.
This means I breathe like you do,
only I have a compulsion to notice
and write it down. In case you forget.
I write it down for both of us.
Single parent, raising two children—
everything happens in singles now.
Poems in single lines.
Line by line.

A slice of cheese.
Toilet paper.
A single free minute to jot this down.
God, I hope this poem never ends,
I feel so alive. Which reminds me,
here is what I wanted to tell you—
I took the kids to the park yesterday.
We flew their kite. The day had wind.
The kite soared. I mean, it really soared!
Upon holding the end of the string,
I was overcome with the pull
of immense sadness. I realize this sounds stupid,
but there's something I'm trying to get at here.
I became aware that the kite too was tugging
toward freedom. So, naturally, I had no choice
but to let it go. My therapist says, letting go
is the practice. Who am I to keep anything?
I watched it sail over the rooftops
and blend in with the clouds, far beyond
our vision. This did happen.
It wasn't just a kite of imagination.
Who's got time for metaphors?
The kids screamed, cussed at me, actually,
for doing this. Said they'd never forgive me,
as they stormed back to the truck.
Hell yes, it was worth it.
Nothing so beautiful as watching
a kite sail off, untethered.
As watching your kids
sail off, untethered.
Nothing so beautiful

as letting go. I'd do it again.
Let go the string.
I'm doing it now.

7.22.20

Salvador now owns a football that throws itself back at you.
Children have become masters of solitude games.
In the future there will be a wellspring of artists, no doubt.
Untouchable and socially awkward, but brilliant with a brush.
Video games too rule the day. Virtual circles of loosely
defined friends, kids and adults who have never met,
conquering a common evil, shouting into a TV screen.
We sat at a cliff last night, the kids and I, and all the stars
were below us. I take it back, we are not the stars,
only the darkness that surrounds. And those glimmering lights,
millions of them—inventory of our wounds.

We will remember this.

THIS CITY

Has all the metaphors built into it.
It's where one family comes to end a life.
It's where the same family comes to begin.
And it's been this way for centuries.
Two hours ago I held you
And I've come to realize something crucial.
It's impossible to write a love poem while standing in this city.
Not if you're being real with yourself.
Which is the only way to write a love poem.
You can write a *fuck you* poem here.
Even a seduction poem, maybe.
Things can take place here.
You can lose yourself.
I lost it here. Once. Strike that. Twice.
It's impossible to belabor a sentiment in this city.
The people strive for something real.
Here, both sides of everything matter
It's never either / or.
For instance, you've been two hours gone now,
and I've been two hours silenced.
By the last words you said to me:
Love is never enough.
This city is an intersection.
No, wait, that was me. I said, *Love is never enough.*
What matters is that it was said.
Two hours have come and gone—
There's no need for symbolism.
Look, this city isn't a sentiment,

nor does its name mean "The Passing."
Just as I wrote this a dust storm clouded
the best part of my idea.
So, I'm left again, two hours now, indecisive
about the direction.
Dirt gets into all the parts here.
I think it will take a new rumor to be cleared of it.
In which the truth is neither here nor there.
In which both sides refuse
To listen to the other.

REFRACTION #3

Romantic love

just isn't the same anymore.
We throw out the garbage, and return
into the cold house with a craving for tuna.
Stare out the window of this year,
at other people's lives, and suddenly it's noon,
and the feral cat brings a dead pigeon to your door
—it's the sexiest offering in months.
The mailman waves hello from a safe distance,
leaving nothing in your box but want.
Thank the Gods you're done with jealousy and pettiness.
The garbage, the window, a lifeless bird
—things you can count on.
Learn to be at peace with peace, a lover once told me.
They tell me there's even a word for it, *ennui*.
Just like the French to fuck up
a perfectly good emptiness.

8.18.20

Addiction. It's you again.
Didn't I last leave you in a hotel parking lot in Fort Stockton?
God, you looked like a gem. You always did. We touched
beneath the dinner table. Whispered I love you in the dark.
That was the last of it.

I've already forgotten.

SELF PORTRAIT AT 46

He once farted in his sleep and woke up angry
    that he lost a dream.
He feels sentimental about white hair not his.
He still finds reasons to rebel against straight lines.
For instance, his eyeglasses, he hates that they get in the way
    of being clearly.
In a desert town, he cohabitates with a reptile, two humans,
    and a headful of visitors.
He once fell off the cliff of a sidewalk in Boulder, Colorado,
    and it felt like love.
He goes for a walk, and when he returns he wishes he could
    take it all back.
When in Fresno he does not trust doctors
    without business cards.
He is the son of a truck driver who once discovered
    an endless road.
He once mistook beer for love and was grateful
    they never married.
He sits in silence until he can't stomach the noise.
When in El Paso he does not trust curanderas
    with business cards.
He hasn't seen a barber in 25 years.
He misses the sound his hair makes when it hits the ground.
He is nostalgic about the shadows his body keeps releasing.
He remembers to water the plants but forgets
    to water himself.
He taught his children to make owl sounds with their hands,
    then regretted it.

Every time a guest arrives they ask the same question.
He once prided himself on making beautiful things from shit.
For years his lover shit on him, and he replied, *That's beautiful!*
Each morning he drinks a green holy powder that's said to
    cure the debt.
He can speak to his aging mother now without the resentment
    of being born.
If he blushes when naked, his body looks like
    an elongated turnip.
He never looks in the mirror—unless he has a craving
    for turnips.
Which is never, because he doesn't eat plants, he only
    drinks them in a green powder.
And this only happens once a day, which is about
    how long he exists anymore.

TIME CAPSULE

Sitting on my porch, I opened
a copy of Creeley's *Life & Death*
and found an old receipt, just now:

October 11, 2010, 12:14 pm
Arsenio's Mexican Food
Fresno, California
Order #0022
1 Special #20 $4.82

It's likely, that day, I was on my way
to the county dump, where in a moment,
I was to deposit, a truckload of refuse
we no longer needed. We were moving back
to Colorado around that time, but who really knows?
That's what we told ourselves. In truth,
we were only moving closer to the Great Divide.
What is clear is that I ordered only one
special this day. No drink. It was noon.
What was I thinking? A Monday.
I consulted the calendar just now.
I want to forget things as they actually happened.
In consideration of numerology, why all these
twos and ones and zeros between us?
And why would it take Creeley,
on a porch, overlooking the Rio Grande,
to discover that on October 11, 2010, I was ordering
one special #20. And when it was gone,

it was gone. I still have heartburn. This receipt,
the only evidence of where I was,
or might've been. At the very bottom,
just above the torn edge,
a most unsentimental poem written,
as if by your hand:
Gracias por venir!

8.30.20

Rumi practices ballroom dancing in her bedroom,
in front of a mirror that she trusts. She perfects
the foxtrot with a computer screen.
Off and on, a song slips from beneath her door.
These are the days of her shy guitar. She emerges
from her room, and declares, I am now 16!
The way the passing ambulance declares,
One more body for the night!
Sal is reading The Diary of Anne Frank *now.*
A moment ago, before he dozed off, with eyes half shut,
he whispered to me, Why did she want a boyfriend, Dad?
Didn't she know she could love anybody?

I must remember this.

LIMERENCE

When the aroma of it was nothing
but a distant reckoning, he wrote
a poem for a woman—
an embroiderer of various strands.

It went:
You looked at me once with the still
gaze of a newborn. Goddamn,
everyone should know what that feels like.

No, the poem went:
I once laid down in the bed of a pickup truck
and smoked a hand-rolled cigarette
in the parking lot of Casa de Fruta
I sang for you then as I sing for you now,
I've lived in this desert too long!

No, the poem wasn't about distance. It went:
I don't write poems anymore. Who cares.
No one ever reads the laugh lines on the mouth
of a dying man. When you and I are in a room
together, well, I can only imagine
that this must be the way an apple feels
when no one is hungry.

Nothing was the poem. There was no poem.
No wall. No apple. No house of fruit.
She tried convincing him

of the privilege and duty.
He admitted it was all a lie, a trap.
He had only meant to win her affection.

Whatever made it to the page was
a record of it. All ideas of entanglement
exist this way. Just as a poem is an idea
of connections that do and do not exist.
Anyway, he wrote one.
He read it to himself.
It went:

And it was gone.

UNQUALIFIED POEM

For Joshua Rubin and Amiri Baraka

I.

Today is November 21, 2018, and last night
150 adolescent girls were transported
into Tornillo Children's Detention Facility
because they do not *qualify*
to be released to their parents.
Thanksgiving is tomorrow, and I am writing to you
from my home in El Paso,
where I just had a mushroom omelet, coffee, and two figs
with a human who swore she loved me.
Where I can hold my son, Salvador, and kiss him now
if I want to. He might smell like old milk,
but this poem doesn't care. Not like I do.
This poem—and its friends—will point its fingers
and deny this to be true. But right now
I have a combined total of $1.47 in my bank account
and there is nothing this poem can do about it.
I couldn't sell this poem if I wanted to.
Even if I could, this poem would be indifferent.
It cannot march into the gates of Tornillo,
or croon to incarcerated children carols at Christmas,
demand ~~300~~, 800 be returned to their families.
This poem has no legs or mouth. You may argue
that it does, but has it ever sipped coffee in the blue rains
of Asheville, North Carolina, while in soft conversation
with a woman it was not allowed to fall in love with?

Have you ever been kissed by a poem? It's true—
it cannot exist without you or I, but don't mistake that
for caring. Because a poem has no heart. A child has a heart.
A poem is neither alive nor dead. It lives on white sheets,
or on the breath of you and I. But a poem itself
cannot breathe. It doesn't *qualify*
as human. There are now ~~800~~, 1,800 children, cold
and huddled inside Tornillo, just forty miles away
from this poem, but it doesn't matter, because this poem
cannot offer them their mother's arms. Though it will argue
that it can. It may even attempt to stretch itself.
Or later, further down the road, decide to
celebrate itself and sing itself. It will ask you
to assume so much. But don't let it fool you.
A poem will never caress you, even if it promises
all the love. Poems love to promise
all the love. But it's incapable of it.
Just ask the ~~1,200~~ 2,000 *unqualified*
children inside Tornillo if poems care.
They might shrug. Children have eyes
and fingers, flesh and feet, with which they
kick soccer balls over fences. Soccer balls care
about as much as poems. Both are circular
and kicked around for sport. Both can hurl fences.
Right now ~~2,000~~ 1,500 children are desperate
to make a phone call, holding on
for dear life. But this poem will never make
that connection. This poem is all talk—
don't let it seduce you.

II.

My children live here in Texas with me.
Their mother lives in California.
This poem is incapable
of carrying them to her. It's not a vehicle.
Today is now December 4, 2018
and they cannot touch their mother.
Not even with a poem. You think they haven't tried?
Last night, my son climbed into bed with me.
We cuddled, and I rested my mouth
against the back of his head, inhaling him deeply.
In that short contact between
his scent and my nose, I could not help
but wonder how distance shapes us.
In two weeks they will fly to visit her.
My children are *qualified* to travel alone.
Days ago I took them both to Tornillo.
We met a man named Joshua Rubin—
a software developer from Brooklyn.
He's been posted at the gates, bearing
witness for months now. I explained
to the children what this meant.
But why, dad?
Because accountability.
Someone who wasn't there
will tell the story and get it wrong.
Joshua knows this. He's left his job
to be here. For children
he does not know. Has never met.
Morning to night. He misses
his wife. Their longing is nothing

compared. One day these tents
will come down, and this land
will return to what it was. We cannot forget
the children who cried out
the names of their mothers and fathers
from the silent desolation of this desert.
Children who shat themselves
for fear of the faceless machine, who lost
their breath while standing in line,
an eternity, waiting to become *qualified*.

III.

Joshua Rubin documents:
> *Four BCFS buses were seen leaving*
> *the airport, carrying passengers*
> *They have arrived at Tornillo.*
> *Hundreds more children carried in.*

> *150 girls brought in as*
> *prisoners last night.*

> *They are heedless of my eyes on them,*
> *they are unashamed, nobody besides*
> *myself and a few others point out to*
> *them that they are doing something*
> *wrong, and I don't know if they ever*
> *doubt themselves. Do they even suspect*
> *they are involved in a crime against*
> *humanity?*

IV.

It is now January 2019, frigid, 20's at night.
Days ago, Joshua approached the fence
and spoke to a few children, but he was threatened
away by the guards. He tells us, each morning,
just before sunrise, you can hear
thousands of birds, cackling and singing
across the cotton fields. Nature has memory.
But let me remind you, the poem doesn't care.
If it cared, as it often claims, it would grow legs
and walk off this page, hitchhike to
the *Marcelino Serna Port of Entry,*
and stand at the stone gates with Joshua Rubin.
Make itself useful. But this poem cannot
hitchhike because it has no thumbs.
No eyes. And to witness you need eyes to see,
ears to record. There are now ~~1,500~~ 3,000 children
locked inside a prison at Tornillo, Texas.
Today is Tuesday, and you are here,
maybe on your couch, maybe at a café,
reading a book of poems. But this doesn't *qualify*
as a poem. Joshua Rubin is perhaps a poem.
~~2,500~~ 2,600 children kicking soccer balls
over a barbed wire fence is a poem.
This is a non-poem; it doesn't care what you think.
It exists forty minutes outside of Tornillo
children's prison, and it will not lift a finger.
Non-poems are like this. They will make promises
but never deliver. It will go on
celebrating itself and singing itself.
It will assume you get these references.
Poems always assume you get their references.

Right now there are ~~2,600~~ 2,800 children
being held captive in a prison, who do not *qualify*
to be reunited with their mothers or fathers.
Right now, you are reading these words,
perhaps in your own home, perhaps
comfortable, near a bedside lamp,
or at your kitchen table, a child at your feet,
wondering silently
whether or not this *qualifies*
as a poem.

9.4.20

How many books did you read this year?
          Only what I purchased.
How many did you purchase?
          Only what I could lose myself in.
How many could you lose yourself in?
          Inside my house there were three bodies.
          In one of them was I lost.
Do you remember any of it?
          I'm remembering now.

REFRACTION #4

Flying

on a paper airplane to California.
Humming over the Continental Divide.
Something unholy about wings as travel.
Turbulent, the nomadic son glides homebound.
Altitude sickness is the angel's revenge.
Or an irrational dream concocted by separation.
With the wind below.
Over endless fields, sprawled like stretch marks
across the belly of valley.
The fog of anticipation limits the view.
Only the heaviest eyes can penetrate.
Two trembling hands origami in consideration.
When the paper unravels, it will be too late.
She sighs, indefinitely, awaiting his arrival.

SETTLING

After Seema Reza

When I am alone, I am almost enough.
I read your lines again, and was reminded
of this. Is it cliché for a man to admit that he's
had his heart broken? More than twice.
This isn't a question, so much as
evidence that my anatomy was once intact.
When I want to feel human
I clip my fingernails and pay attention.
I examined myself in the mirror
just this morning, after a hot shower,
and discovered that my chest appears
to be saying, *I don't believe in love anymore.*
What can I tell you? I have eaten the
insides of oysters, and learned
the hard way: No one can force a pearl
before it's time. I painted
my toenails black, while staring
adoringly at a blank canvas.
It was perfection. I could see it all.
The toilet hissed, and I hissed back.
When her house would creak,
my grandmother would say, "It's settling."
It runs in the family, this business
of settling. I'm up to twelve houseplants now,
but none of them choose green.
When I am alone, I am almost enough.
I am almost wholly there.

A moment ago, I cooked a pot of water,
and grew nostalgic for figs.
God bless the slaughter of wasps
that bequeath their lives to the pulp.
Who wouldn't want sweetness to be
their dying legacy? I looked up
the etymology of solitude. It showed
a photo of a house, settling.
I stood at the window of it, and caught
my own redemption. It was almost
enough. When left to my own vices,
I become arrogant, and make pacts
to forget what she tastes like. Untie
all the shoes and pull the tongues
loose. Hike all the switchbacks
between these bookshelves,
and the mountain of photographs
that will never see light.
As long as I am here now,
in this deserted city,
I may as well bring myself to the party.
If I'm not enough, I'm not.
But if I am, you can bury this poem
under the house, settle
this thing once and for all.

9.22.20

Clarity.

Clarity.

Clarity.

I must remember this.

SANDALWOOD

This morning, I had considered buying stock
in sandalwood, but then I read that stock
in sandalwood has gone up, since India
has designated the heartwood tree endangered,
and thieves in the bush, with high-powered machines,
and access, who know the underworlds, have figured
out ways to quietly, delicately, hack the trees,
and haul off truckloads, yielding $4,000 per.
The Australians got in on this too.
The down-under was capable of tricking
the seed to take earth. And prices stabilized,
until the sting. The sandalwood gang had disappeared
over 20 tons of Heartwood. There was a shootout
in Jakarta, 12 men were killed. Three bystanders.
No children. These are sandalwood wars.
Not the essence of wars. What kind of desperation,
to stain the Heartwood with human blood,
only to have it end up on the market?
The authorities burnt an immense pyre
of Heartwood, to send a message to the thieves.
But the aroma was intoxicating, and immediately
recognized across the region. That night, without
hesitation, every lover knew what would take place.
The children have since been born, and are recycled
into a life of sandalwood. It is a terrible obsession,
I have. Each morning, after I bathe,
I dab my finger into the golden oil, and place

the essence of it on my person. And, like this,
I walk boldly into the tasks of my day, feeling
at such immense peace with myself, and with
the interconnection of all things.

SALVADOR

We've been sharing a bed for months now
And I wonder, if like married couples,
two people who sleep touching
over a length of time, end up taking on
traits of the other, then what parts of us
are becoming one as we sleep?
Perhaps I'll wake up tomorrow with a dance
germinating in my thighs. Perhaps you'll wake up
with stubble and acid reflux. Somewhere,
between a snore and a fart, you are contemplating
the weight of fatherhood. Tomorrow
the alarm clock will ring, and we will wake up,
father and son staring, into the other silently,
like two moose in a meadow.
I might claim to know some things about you.
Desires you aren't even aware you have.
You'll claim to know some things about me.
History I was sure I've hidden. When we brush
our teeth, it is our teeth we brush. When you
wash your hands, it's your grandfather's
ashy knuckles that soften. I pay attention
to the way you part your hair now.
It's such a delicate motion. I want to tell you,
Keep that beauty for yourself. Don't give it
away. But we both know that's impossible.
We are here to fall. And we are here

to scrape ourselves off the slate. We are here
to give it all away. Crawl back into bed.
Carry what's left of ourselves
toward a dream.

10.10.20

Tonight, again, the feral cats wail and fuck
and claim their cactus beneath my bedroom window.
It's a prickly season. Sleep deprived, and this
incurable loneliness. The election brings
good distraction. This is our year, everyone says.
It's our turn. But we still float our kisses.
Host drive-by birthdays. Reconsider our circle—
those we love, and why we love them. We decide
whether or not to love again. Our arms
can only stretch so far. We have our groceries
delivered now. No need to walk the aisles.
Don't handle the utensils! And don't stare at me
through the glass door. No one wants to touch anymore,
but we all want to be held. We walk around sanitized.
Distance, *the Father says, to the virtual congregation,*
is the new compassion.

We must remember this.

THE POET'S RETURN

For Luis Humberto Valadez

Chicago Heights never rolled soft.
A quiet thrush in the sewers awaits.
Like when we last strolled beneath the "L."
Talked about foreign currency and dreams.
Lu Yi, arriving with the step of a newborn.
Years later, I stood at the toe of Innisfree.
Where I found you folded neatly.
Between the covers, before the sour dedication
you wrote: *I will be gone.*
I might return again.
A gray lull about you that day.
Like when you almost ended the sentence.
In a bottle of warm vodka.
And I found you, broad shoulders slumped.
Both ears, turned upward, a pair of turtle shells wading.
Lu Yi returns from a life in Neijiang, some will say.
Lu Yi arrives with a pocketful of ashes.
Your last poem before exit.
A few of us will gather.
Those who understand the weight of your smile.
Maybe there will be a meal, colorful vegetarian dishes.
Together we will eat and talk.
Lu Yi will open his eyes to the shadow of a home.
And I can hear you say, to no one, out loud,
Everyone deserves to be written about, sometimes.

REFRACTION #5

They Are Flying Their Flags

them neon bloods, waving brash slogans,
chanting *greatness* in the name of Country
a banner on every corner, erections of idolatry,
all hail to the king of convenience.
What is this strange fascination with garment, and colors?
What religion have we made of shape and shadow?
We could burn them all and still it would not be enough
fire to warm the family.
Give me something lasting, unfurl your frightened side.
Tell me, when you kiss, who exactly are you kissing?
Where inside your body do you cage the child?
Fuck this fear of sentiment, abstractions are all
anyone is made up of anyway.
Go ahead, drag the message across
the windshield of narrow machines,
but don't lie to me about loss, rather,
wave the banner of who you love in the time you love them.

10.19.20

The air lacks romance.
Have I said this before?
How can we forget?
It's all anyone looks for anymore.
That and childcare.
And toilet paper.
And the definition of "essential."
I can hear the monks cry out—
                       Everything is essential!
In time, it will be essential
that we remember this.

HOMETOWN ODE

For Destina Unica and Dezyrae Amor

Visalia—where first the necessity of words found me
Had never known myself to be
Until Slick Rock spit me out
Until I handed you my life in groves and acrid blossoms
Until you split my heart like this
Until my tooth punctured though the bottom lip
Let's count the broken bones, a clavicle and other structures
Visalia, no wonder Steinbeck ratted you out
When I'm with you, I long for elsewhere
When I'm elsewhere, I long for plums
Your streets can still hold me
But your telephone wires go on disappointing the birds
We had baseball in April, and that was all
It seems you get along alright without me
I won't express to you my illusions
And all these scars without a story
And 200,000 eyes without a bookstore
Cannot read the rings around Kaweah Lake
I didn't forget about Virgil
Or the steady black nostril of your Glock
I simply forgave you
I've been trying hard to write you out of my head
But the line of cars at Mooney's Grove Park on Easter Sunday
    still plays our song
What have I left out?
That I was once a drunken wreck on the shoulder
    of Lover's Lane

On the night that cowboy blew his skull
Or that I sought solitude in your walnut groves in winter
I still can't pass Sequoia High School without feeling
    sentimental about barbed wire
You must wonder why your children left
What else?
Oh yes, the one about a kid, who thought one day
he might return to speak openly with you
Calling it poetry

ISH

I tell them they can expect me around 9-ish.
Rumi says to me, Are you sure, or just sure-ish?
I say, I'm sure-ish.
Because this is the most accurate after all.
If for instance I were to say, I will arrive at 9 on the dot,
and I happen to arrive at 8:59, then I would be a liar.
If I arrived at 9:01 the same would apply.
Even if I arrived at 9 on the dot,
and the clock on the television was a minute slow,
I would still be inaccurate.
Accuracy is an illusion, I say to my children,
and to anyone who will listen.
It is for mathematicians and engineers, and even then,
there is still an *ish* factor to contend with.
Which is more accurate—
The illusion of accuracy?
Or the acknowledgment of inaccuracy?
Therefore, everything is *ish!*
You could say, for instance, this is not a poem.
Yet, it appears in some poetic form.
It doesn't rhyme. There is no stanza.
Only language blob.
It is a poem only because I am telling you
it is a poem. Is and isn't.
Ish is and isn't.
An in-between place
of history and possibility.
If I tell you to expect me at 9-ish,

what I am really saying is,
I will be there, mostly,
though part of me will stay behind,
which part is to be seen,
but even so, when the clock
strikes on the hour-ish,
I promise to be present,
in the most recent form of myself,
on time and whole-ish,
if you'll wait for me.

11.2.20

How do you build an altar
for Year of the Dead?
There aren't enough marigolds
to pretty it up. 229,000 lights
in search of a saint.
The ofrenda is built inside
the Convention Center,
made of street lamps and sirens,
and a thousand empty beds, praying
for inoculation.
Kiss the tomb of your beloved
from behind a veil.
Even breath requires distance,
unless exhaled in a strip club.
Nothing more essential
than a dollar bill,
wedged between lips.
There will be sugary skulls,
cardboard gatherings, and other
elected ornaments. We have only one
day to make it happen,
to bury the past, and call upon
the ghosts who bear our name.
And they are counting on us
to get it right.

TIK TOK

She reads
Rebecca Solnit
She reads
Cheryl Strayed
She watches videos of
Chimamanda Ngozi Adichie,
Tik Toks of women
dancing on tombs
of the patriarchy
She doesn't eat animals
because she's lost too many, as it is
She delivers speeches
on esoteric subjects,
Anzaldúa's *Nepantla*,
the divisiveness of rhetoric,
calls out the hypocrisy
of prayer, and *rednecks*,
calls out her brother's misuse
of the word *favoritest,*
and then convinces him
to start a band.
Yesterday, she bought her own clothes
a package arrived at the door,
she tried them on before a mirror
liked what she saw,
emerged from her room
and said, out loud to no one,
I'm really feeling myself today!

And for an instant,
I watched her standing, in her own
natural light.
It's late winter,
I love her,
I don't know how long
this desert can hold us,
but it's worth
the wonder.

BROWN LOTUS (A PERFORMANCE)

—a mediocre contortionist,
       smuggled in the glove compartment
         of a '57 Chevy
           I arrived
             one foot in the ass cheeks
               the other folded beneath armpit
           like a catcher's mitt
Used to be that I daydreamed
         in a narrow canoe
           on the floral waters of Xochimilco,
       back when bees congregated in wax cathedrals
                 & lit veladoras
                   until military blew 'em out.
In Tajik teahouses I enter
      the kitchen in search
         of the brew master,
           slicing ginger thin, cardamom in molcajete,
            because he is my father,
               from the forgotten green of
                       Michoácan,
dressed in worn jeans
      & baseball cap that reads Cruz Azul,
         blew across Nogales
        in a canteen of cactus pulp,
          a Swiss wristwatch
            set to Mountain Time,
              arrived in a Colorado tavern

near Raton Pass
in search of The Buffalo
and wound up a Sherpa
for the gringos who paid cash
to free climb the Grand Teton.

It's true—
I empathize
with the crime of wire
twisted & left   to corrugate
& take blame for delineations
only man conjures.

I am the bastard child you left
hunkered on a coffee can
                    —I'll say
promised you'd send for me in a year,
dummied up the papers
and sold them in Greeley
to the cousin of a meat packer
snatched up in an ICE sting
                    —I'll say
I'm the meat forgotten
turning rancid
in Tombstone Park
                    —I'll say
among the pollos
whose eyes still see
long after the legs
have run off with the body
                    —Don't ask if
                         I'm illegal

the forgotten son,
heartbreak of Olmec proportions,
    I am the one who bought out all the intestines
    and monopolized the industry
    of underground roach-coaches,
this in the millennium summer,
    it's true, no money was ever exchanged
    I performed the disembowelment
    ceremony with my own two hands,
    the paper mistook it for a crop circle
    but it was an old Nahuatl joke.

Now I've got a sitcom
    each week a million faces dial in faithfully
    because they know that come Sweeps Week
    after the PBS fund drive
    & before the State of the Union
    we fast in the New Moon
                —or was this Ramadan?

I have visited the great stupa
      looking to mend the wounds
        that I've carried since conception
    about a miracle boy,
      born on the wrong side of Orion,
    seeking answers to the suffering
        synonymous with joy—

I am nothing but a campesino child,
    a brown lotus
    of this post-millennial borderland called t/error.

I was in Afghanistan when the first bomb dropped,
        from an obscure bath house
        I counted down the Year of the Fire Pig,
        the day was a code orange
        when the Spanish subway imploded,

I was prostrating in the bed of an El Camino
        on the outskirts of Coachella
        onion sheers by my side.

I've traveled the world
        believe me when I tell you
        it's all the same.

I was mustard gassed in a Paris train station,
        mistook for Moroccan,
        it was World Cup season after all
        and the canines were in full regalia.

A friend once told me to never turn my back on the dogs
        so everywhere I go now
        I do so in reverse—

        This is how I'll remember
        the ghost waters of the San Joaquin River
    fading
        How I will remember
        Chautauqua Park,
        kneeling out beyond the Great Plains
        in devotional pose
    fading

How I will remember
the still egret standing
in the awful silence of snow

fading

How I will remember
your rough hands combing the vortex
of hair above my scalp,
a penetrable wall,
through which our dreams were visible,
everything about us

fading

11.11.20

The spike in numbers reads like a barometer
of our will to survive. Today we are up
813 bodies. Yesterday it was 1,600.
Rise and fall with the red line. We oscillate.
I hate my life. I love my life. They are one in the same.
Still, sides are being chosen. How far we have slipped
is measured by the number of conversations we have
with ourselves. But what can I do about this?

                              You can cry.
But is crying enough?
                              Have you ever cried out loud,
                              in public, before?
I have.
                              But did you track the journey of your
                                                          tears?
Yes, I did. I did.
                              Did you taste the salt?
                              Ask questions of it?
Excuse me?
                              If you haven't cried like this,
                              then you haven't cried hard enough.
                              An unexamined cry is not worth its salt.

                              Remember this.

HER MAJESTY'S LAST STAND

For Toñita Morales, Yolanda Leyva, David Dorado Romo, Veronica
Carbajal, Paso Del Sur, and my great-grandmother Nicolasa Flores

We call it *Duranguito*,

it's two steps

from the port of entry—

The Birthplace of El Paso

it is said, leads

to a dead end,

a duel, West Texas style,

between history

and progress,

now corralled by tornado

fence and adobe

mounds, busted brick   memories

lost on the dollar—

Where once

newspapers reported

of *Amazon women*

leading a revolt

in Juárez bathhouses,

broken beer bottles

and civil disobedience,

where the ghost of 17-year-old

Carmelita Torres

still rises

in fumigation mist,

blankets over Overland Street—

Where in the Villa years,

atop hotels, war voyeurs,

sipped tea, and witnessed

revolution,   if mortar could talk,

if bone and stone

could bellow
Cucurrucucú Paloma

to coax white Jesus

down from brown Cristo Rey,

he would no doubt

find his way

to Doña Tonita's blue sidewalk

bench, pecked clean

by filial pigeons,

and bow to kiss

the holiness of her

majesty's last stand—

This is what exists
in the air above Duranguito,

if place holds memory,

then Toñita's trembling hands

are the unrecorded

testimonies of the incarcerated

children whose artwork

lines her street—

Alone, she towers,

maybe five feet

nothing   unassuming

the solitary white

haired Doña, overshadowing

the statue of Oñate's

castrated horse, sweeping

dust from her home,

which is this neighborhood,

which is your neighborhood too,

until it isn't—

But you've heard this story before—

old woman,

stands up

to greedy oligarchs,

guardian of gutted

buildings, matriarch

of crumbling matter,

protests come and go,

no suit wants to be

the one to break her

before the cameras,

so she goes on,

outliving the story,

with one good eye,

fifteen feral cats,

and her slow broom,

night after night,

ushering all the dirt

of the city

back into the light.

VARIATIONS ON *THIS LAND*

This land is your land,
this land is Comanche land,
Mescalero Apache land,
Coahuiltecan land, my ancestors—
bent to build the Alamo, then slaughtered
and buried beneath it, risen again, to be forgotten,
now a river to be walked upon, treaded by tourists,
on a mission, who find San Antonio a city
with two thighs, good only for entering and exiting.
This land is my grandfather's land
whipped to suffer his color in the cumin air,
to erase that he ever loved, the way only a brown boy
can love Brownsville, beneath oil derricks
and sugarcane horizons, and fields
of afterthought, a cluster of cancerous
lovers in the wake of red dust, and pickup truck
envy, never again, this land, never—
This Land looks better in the rearview,
better under night's speckled eye,
better in the black sputum
of its horny oceanic spills, better under
the fog of hurricanes, or the distant plano-myth
of its own romantic promise, this land
is your Matanza land, your prideful legacy
of mounted Rangers by dawn's zealot light land,
mass unmarked graves, and tales of a nascent Amerika
on the come up, your Corpse of Christ land,
that tore the tongue from my grandmother's

tender jaw, this is your inheritance, not the land
but the stories of land, *this land* is your prideful misnomer,
keep this land, bury yourself here, deep in the heart
of your taxidermied glory, of your nostalgic West,
no amount of sermons from your mega-preachers
can undo how vast hexes span.

12.14.20

We have lost
the parents of 545
caged children—
yet, 5G towers
are all the rage.
But can they track down
the families?
We micro-chipped
a monarch butterfly,
and traced it down
to a single tree bough
in Bolivia.
Just yesterday,
NASA's Perseverance Rover
was tasked with locating
ancient microbial life
on Mars—
but we can't locate
non-ancient
human life
on earth?

We must remember this.

REFRACTION #6

There Are 14,000 Starlings

in flight right now, a murmuration no one will ever see.
There are 14,000 rumors still hanging
in the DNA of your fingernail.
There are 280,000 children's teeth to be brushed,
at least 7,000 will fall out.
So many crayons will ignore the lines in a coloring book.
Children in or outside of detention don't color in the lines.
There are 28,000 eyeballs blinking at you.
There, in the center of you, a child is suppressing
their own laughter.
Now, there are only so many days a child
can legally be detained—it's your turn.
As you read this 2,000 of the 14,000 children are still
locked inside the screw.
In Tornillo, Texas, the children spend weeks writing
heartfelt letters to a dumpster.
While my son, Salvador, is playing Xbox and salivating
in high-definition.
And I can play Bob Dylan on repeat and never think twice.
Now I am home, and no amount of words can pick a lock.
Nothing is alright.

SLEEPLESS NIGHTS (THICH NHAT HANH IS DYING)

For Margarita Luna Robles & Juan Felipe Herrera,
Mayela Padilla, Reed Bye, Bobby Byrd (RIP), and Keith Abbott (RIP)

I.

It is Thursday, March 21, 2019,
and Thich Nhat Hanh is dying.
It rained last night and I missed it.
I awoke to two puddles at my doorstep,
and spent the day looking down
to the heavens. My children are in California
again, visiting their mother, and the job now
is to make a good salad—that's it.
I'm considering quitting meat for good, seriously.
Thich Nhat Hanh is dying. I heard he went
back to Vietnam, where his family was killed.
I could never again return to live in Visalia,
where I have had family killed.
Visalia killed Virgil. I'm over it. I am.
But I'm not going back. Visalia is not Vietnam,
I know. And I am not Thich Nhat Hanh.
El Paso is a lonely city. So was Boulder.
At least there were trails to keep me found.
I am lost without a trail.
A woman once told me that in my weakness
I am most strong. I still can't grasp
what that even means. Perhaps I'm not
as weak as she thinks.

II.

It is now Saturday, October 5, 2019,
and I am 45 years old again, and I don't remember
having to clip my fingernails this frequently.
How is it that some bones never give up?
And what is this need to rid myself in tiny ways?
Look at me, so existential at 8:50 a.m.
I quit hallucinating long ago.
I still can't shake the insight. I found something
holy there, and it refuses to let go.
As I've said at least once before, it's suddenly
9:47 p.m., and I am sitting in my truck,
parked in our driveway, Ringold Road,
Texas, planet earth, one galaxy or another,
so what? Thich Nhat Hanh is dying.

III.

While studying at Naropa University,
I took a brushstroke class with Keith Abbott.
My tablemate was a kid named Justin.
We dipped our brushes in the same ink.
Laughed at our clumsy hands. Shared rice paper.
Championed one another's feeble attempts.

>   This is *mū*.
>   This means *is*.
>   This is *is-ness*.
>   Circular stroke.
>   Ensō.

Means *I am here*

            was here

     am here

            returning.

Around this time, my grandfather had just died,
and I got stuck in California. I documented
his last words: *Return the lawnmower to the neighbor.*
He only wanted to do right by people.
When I returned to class, I was told that Justin
would not be returning. In that brief time
I stepped away he had taken his own life.
Justin knew nothing about Vietnam.
Neither did I. And now Keith Abbott is dead too.
This is *mū.*
It means *without.*

IV.

Today is February 2, 2020, and I cannot help
but remember Justin, or Keith, or my grandfather,
and that somewhere in Vietnam, Thich Nhat Hanh
is dying. It scares me, to be *without.* I know Vietnam
is not Visalia. Though people have fled it all the same.
I'm still in exile from who I was in those years.
I'll never return if I can get away with it.
As a young man I considered taking my own life,
genuinely felt it was a benevolent option.
I thought I had lived enough life

to feel complete. It's true.
And just like that it is April again, and they tell me
it is the one year anniversary of the great fire
at the Cathedral of Notre Dame. So what. Somewhere
in heaven Thích Quảng Đức is still kneeling
in contemplation. You weren't even born yet.
Nor was I. Things burn up every day,
doesn't mean we get to shine.

V.

It is now exactly 7:00 p.m.

May 18, 2020,

and Thich Nhat Hanh is somewhere,

at this very moment   dying,

and I am frightened

at the thought of it.

When he goes   who then will hold up

that part of my life?

You've got God.
      I've got glue.
            You've got job security.
            I've got faith.

You've got good looks.

I've got seven prayers

still unanswered.

VI.

Today is Saturday, June 15,
in the Year of the Rat,
and I am reminded of what he said:

We are only a continuation.
We do not die.
We carry on.

If so, then this poem could very well
have been the butterfly that we found
perched on the concrete of our porch
yesterday morning. We fed it water
from a blue cup. It sipped
with its proboscis. The unraveling
is a tricky thing. They call it
reincarnation—but how can we be sure
that isn't just nostalgia
coming back to bite us?

VII.

There are enough anniversaries
to go around. It is now August 3, 2020,

and they are asking us to remember—
Walmart was shot up this day a year ago,
while you were busy writing poems.
23 lives taken—
while you were busy repairing busted sinks.
One of them just a kid—
while you were busy applying makeup
on a perfectly good face.
I've grown tired of altars, so I took the kids
to the skatepark, where we stayed all afternoon.
Did you know, it's the only place
where you can still find kids who aren't seduced
by cell phones? At the skatepark everyone is given
permission to fall. Sometimes, it feels as if all
my dead relatives are staring at me
through cracks in the sidewalks, giving me permission
to fall. Why do I still hold myself accountable
to ghosts? They could skate circles around us.
That same woman once told me that history
has become my identity. Let go
of your history, she said. But four wheels
consistently returning
is what makes the machine go.

VIII.

Here we are,
October 1, 2020,
6:42 p.m., and my children
and I just got back
from a hike
in the Franklin Mountains.

I found an ammonite.
Evidence of the once ocean.
The past finds me. And now
everything happens in twos.
It rained today,
and the scent of the sea
in the air reminded me
that at this very moment
Thich Nhat Hanh is dying.
Only he knows where he's at.
I could never admit to knowing
where I am.
I could only admit
that the scent is my undoing.
Which is to say,
this is where you will find me.
Which is to say,
it is suddenly Thursday,
December 31, 2020,
the eve of a new year,
and they tell me
Thich Nhat Hanh
has not yet left us.

1.2.21

The year has ended,
but the virus persists.
It's claimed its stake,
seized territory of our bodies
and psyches, an assault
of historic proportions.
From the porches of homes and the halls
of institutions, we cry out—
This was supposed to be
a fucking new year! A better year!
But today we were tested.
And I can only think of Janus,
that two faced God,
wanting desperately for the eyes
looking back to close
to all that we have lived, to all
things lost and gone.
What terrible suffering to have
so many eyes in so many directions.
I bolted all the doors shut
and stapled sheets over our windows,
got down on the floor, in the middle
of the living room, and vowed
to sit still until the walls fell away
of their own accord,
—this is how we begin our year.

Waiting for results.

A GROCERY STORE

The apples are so exposed here,
reminding me, I have never been married,
yet, I can't tell you how many aisles
I've walked up and down, and how many cities
I've committed myself to. I'm baffled
by the array of raisins, that still haunts
the men who raised me.
Are these hands mine? This bum knee
that cracked and startled the young lady
examining cucumbers, affectionately?
I've become too aware of my hunger
for honey, and how I've been
avoiding venturing into the meat
section for years now. Ernesto reminds me
I'm on the right path. He challenges me
to return to the gym, but I already fear
the weight I carry. From a magazine rack,
a guru stares at me, her wry smile
suggests I am going about it all wrong,
but Daniel told me it's okay to sometimes
air out the darkness, that it has a purpose.
I've spent years crawling out from under
the spirits aisle, that I find myself now
taking the most comfort in frequenting bars
of soap, and exotic shampoos, organic
facial scrubs not tested on animals.
I buy what I want, what my children need,
find a checkout line with the least resistance

and wait again, until my father drives by
in his diesel. He will stop for a moment,
and in his own tired way, hold me,
like when I was a child, and he was invisible,
a fruit picker, me on his back,
the sun casting down on us,
aisles upon miles of sugar
beets to be weeded.

THE TALK (TALISMAN FOR SALVADOR)

In here, my son—
when I give you consequences, you can trust
it is from love, you can trust
it is not from hatred, or some misdirected
hostility over the angle of your cheekbones,
or because you are invisible
                          & therefore discardable
or because you are too visible
                          & therefore a threat.

Each time I ask you
to pick up after yourself, take you
by the hand, and pull you to the shower,
each time I say to you—

    This is how you properly sweep a floor
    This is how you properly fold your clothes
    This is how you properly make a bed
    This is why you say goodnight,
        why you kiss the cheek for friends,
                and the mouth for love
    Why I tell you, no means no
    because it does.
    This is how you speak to people
    with respect
and your elders with reverence. This is why I cannot
let you get away with small words like *shit*, or *damn*, or *fuck*
and why I practice these words away too,

with great care, and blow it
        at nearly every opportunity.
Because in here you are a loved boy, in here
I will handle you with care and tenderness,
and correct you with purpose, I will allow you the space
to fall and fail, and cry,
and break and hurt and whimper, and ask questions
without answers, and guess without shame,
and live your mistakes out loud, without judgment, and dance
around in your underwear, unabashedly
in love with yourself, and still consider you, in here—

                                        a warrior.

Out there, my son—
love doesn't come
so easily. Out there, they will not exercise
patience with you. Out there, they have made up
their minds about you, out there, they have seen
a hundred boys who look like you, sound like you,
move like you, joke like you, flex like you, smile
like you, and they know exactly what to do
with boys like you. They may have even once been you,
but were never taught their own value,
or didn't have a safe place like *in here*
to turn to when a threat appeared. Out there,
small words like *shit*, or *damn*, or *fuck* will get you
posted at the fence during recess, will get you
a busted lip at the gas pump, get you
chased, get you cornered, get you before a judge—
and say, *Consider yourself lucky*.
Out there, they got no love

for a dark-skinned, brown boy with black hair, black
pupils, and light in his eyes, joy on his face, confident
with his place in the world. Out there, how easily
they forget that you're somebody's son,
and they don't know—how could they?
—that when you were born
you spent three months in a glass case,
with armholes through which we could tickle
your amber skin with fingertips, unable to hold you—
this is how first the world was introduced to you,
at such cruel distance, my God!
To be born into a new realm, unable to grasp
at the familiar? Do they know what irreparable damage
that might've done? All we had then to connect with you
was voice. All we have now is voice. So we sang to you,
your mother and I, whispered good night
and good mornings, and we came to rely on the invisible,
as I am relying on it now.

This is not a poem, nor a prayer, this is in every way
a talisman—

    If I speak this into being, the universe could not be
    so ironic as to target you, these words, this paper
    is my offering, to those maligned deities of fate—
    I present to you this boy of color, this man of color
    this tender and beloved, child of your country
    this youngest brother of three, this son
    to a Mexican mother, and a father who found his way—
    This boy, the endling of Hernandez men, who walks
    the sidewalks and dirt paths as a human worthy of dignity
    Let him walk, let him stumble, let him fall and rise up
        again

Let him carry the burden of his own errors, give him room
To evolve, grow, to shrink, correct himself, take root,
but give him room.

No—
Out there is not in here, my son
Out there, if they call you son, it's not a good thing
Only your mother or I call you son, it means love—
Out there they will not call you by name, will not
honor the history of your three regal syllables:

>Sal—salt of earth, your inheritance

>Va—to go, fly

>Dor—the opening, an invitation, walk through

Say it with me—Salvador.

Will they know it means savior?

Will you know?

Are you listening to me?

2.10.21

One door opens, another door
is a window, depends on which day.
Some days we live by law, other days
by rumor. It comes and goes.
A pendulum we dodge
when it swings our way.
A jump rope. Careful
not to catch our necks.
It's true, I have given up
plenty of people
this past year. Redefined
the meanings of things.
For instance, bacon
is no longer aligned with me
spiritually. I can no longer
fathom eating the angel.
I won't fall back. I have
given up the falseness,
and the facade. If it isn't
unmasked, it isn't for me.
I love finding the music
in the grass, and making things
of clouds. I still set spiders free.
I am attuned to bees
more than people. No matter
how dark the quarantine, we must
always remember, we still contain,
perhaps not all, but at least
—some of the light.

NATURAL TAKEOVER OF
SMALL THINGS

. . . surrounded by bones, surrounded by cells,
by rings, by rings of hell, by hair, surrounded
by air-is-a-thing . . .

—Jack Collom, *Ecology*

HOME

Fresno is the inexhaustible nerve
in the twitching leg of a dog
three hours after being smashed
beneath the retread wheel
of a tomato truck en route to
a packing house that was raided
by the feds just days before the harvest,
in which tractors were employed
to make do where the vacancy
of bodies could not, as they ran out
into the oncoming traffic of Highway 99,
arms up in dead heat, shouting
the names of their children,
who were huddled nearby,
in an elementary school, reciting
out loud, *The House That Jack Built*.

BROWN CHRIST

Yesterday, I saw God,
a Brown Christ hovering
above an onion field
over tilled plains of the San Joaquin—
frayed constellation of denim,
ox hide work boot broken at the heel,
a curved knife gripped in his fingers,
low clouds undulating, hair of broken
lemongrass & rodeo lasso,
a fragrant beard of perejíl,
everything smelled of sulphur
& manure, the silos wept
and snowflakes tumbled tenderly
from the day moon, refracting
luminous congregations of aspen,
with the music of truck dogs
howling over accordions,
shimmering manna-light.

THE DAY JOHNNY TAPIA DIED ON MY SIDEWALK

was the same as yesterday. A cart crammed
with Mexican pastries, a man beneath blue umbrella
calling out, *Mayonesa!* Out front the barren lawn,
the pit bull chained to fence post, lapping its testicles
and griping at the sun.

The church bell rang and the school bell rang.
Both bells rang in concentric circles that rose up and skimmed
the bellies of the departing planes that disrupted
the satellite discs over the houses sagging on Kenmore Drive,
where girls in tight jeans walked hand in hand with boys
in tighter jeans. Krylon-sprayed ball caps cocked to studded
ear lobe, sideburns trimmed to a blade.

Across the street, McLane High was pep rallying
to the instrumentation of brass and skin, while worn
stadium lights spilled dimly down Clinton Avenue.
The football team was dressed and counting down
the kickoff. The weed eater buzzed next door.
On the front porch children practiced dance moves to a pop
tune, outdated. Across the street, campesinos bumped
Ramon Ayala's early days, about a corner in the sky, snapped
open cold bottles of X on the driveway, and stood around
flexing, arguing over who was more Mexican than the other.

UNDELIVERED POSTCARDS TO LYDIA

I don't want to see you now or ever in monsoon pesadilla
anchored to plasma tendrils & radiation, tumbleweed
stricken between old Socorro & injected skins of the San
    Joaquin.
I never wanted these things for you—
la pisca on a never-ending vine, stretching the horizon,
to a sagging army barrack in Korea, your father blowing
Woody Guthrie in harmonic shrapnel sandwiches, discharged
for government cheese and bad piñones, while the
    bougainvillea
eavesdrops on the windowsill, pretending
not to listen.

*

I am here now, on the shadow side of the Rocky Mountains,
weighted by papers, contemplating the soft tooth
of a wolf spider hunkered in the sycamore, perched on the
    banks
of a rivulet, until I can no longer decipher the beats
of my own breath, from the intoxication of unnamed insects
sexing in the fragrant willow.

*

Lydia, I have heard that there are cemeteries in Socorro
where headstones are kept clean by iguanas with tiny fingers,
whose tongues are immune to the scorpion's sting.

Socorro!

Where you found your sister in a methamphetamine dream,
later to hallucinate ghetto birds in Bakersfield boneyards.

Socorro!

Where neutron bombs blossom over the Sandia Mountains,
and molecules are still recovering from the eternal blush
of deafening red.

Socorro!

What have I left out? Boyle Heights? Dinuba? A left breast?

The Great Horned Owl hunkered in the sycamore?

*

What does it matter?
In the end they will say, Lydia.
Who throws lamps at her children and tames them
with broomsticks. Lydia who wails for barefoot babies with
    dirty faces.
Little Lydia with her brother's jeans. Lydia of Deming, New
    Mexico.
Lydia of Roma. Of East Los Angeles. And of the gardens
in the suburbs. They will say Lydia who dropped out. Lydia
    who married
the gangster. Lydia with the white face and thin lips, who
    swears
by astrology but doesn't tell God. Lydia with the harvested
    lymph nodes.

Lydia bowing in the groves. Lydia in an open field of alfalfa.
Lydia whose eyes turn auburn in sunlight. Lydia who mothers
other people's children. Lydia with a gift of listening.
Lydia with a gift for you. They will say Lydia was my mother.
    That Lydia,
the woman who was paranoid about the end. Lydia who had
    a book
written in her head. Lydia whose son took the kids and fled.
    Lydia
with biceps like warm dough. Lydia who kept birds-of-
    paradise
on the kitchen table. Lydia who delighted in old avocados in
    bread.
Lydia whose epitaph will read: just don't forget me. There
    goes Lydia
they will say, I was lucky to have been held by her.

SAN JOAQUIN SUTRA

Valley of Saints,
    where holy preachers and Night Train drunk vagrants
      hobble their limbs in Oval Park,
where once Lincoln's beard got served
      the wasted pulpo of seven seas
      and the people lit up dazzling lights on Christmas Eve,
      where in mud ditches
bathe the nude brown children
        & broken whites
    who together learned to speak crawdad
      in irrigation pipes,
    barefoot on busted wine bottles,
      and when days extend their radiant arms
      they follow the river into the mouth
      and there again
      learn to become mountain child
    bulked like trunks of redwood trees,
where campesino grandfathers bait little ones
    with raw serrano peppers
    teaching them early
to memorize flavors of pain
    how the eyes flood, and the tongue is left
      to burn in silence,
where tractor stoned youth chuck dirt clots at the testicles of bovines
    just to watch them giddy up their asses
      in frightening masks, toppling the massive beasts
    from their heavy hooves,
      guzzling gun powder in bulge tight
      denims and ostrich hide roach killers

laughing at the cosmos lyric
in the radio box beaming
satellite signals across Scorpio's crab hands,
out among the celestial
expansion of the widest brim yet,
where stands a jail cell for every son, two for paroled transients
who sleep along drought stricken streams
beneath totemic overpasses
xylophone of ribs
ballad for bread
kneeling in shadows of Dairy Land factories and packing sheds
that reek of bruised fruit,
mutiny bourgeoning   among the cashews.

*

I was there
in the vicious freeze of '98
wearing eggplant colognes & indestructible trousers,
stationed beneath burning oil heaters,
fanning the night with my holy hands
when salt rock bullets entered the flesh
and I experienced the first death—

Sacred valley of Kaweah rivers,
crooked horse legs creaked in crimson,
valley of thigh and crotch,
sacred lake of tule foliage
fossilized in conch shells and holy stalagmite,
—everything here sacred, you see
the ditch banks and mass choirs alike,
pious families and albino eyed field mice
snarling at the sky,

                    the foxtails and abandoned dogs of the countryside
                            wagging tongues
                                        in dead air,
                        sacred mariachi girth
                        and carp scales lost in teeth,
                        finger plucking catgut,
            smooth river   rock and fungal gutters
                            and neon waters trickling in the chasm,
                        sacred the young mothers and fathers—that never were
                        the black moon of a mechanic's fingernail,
            the silos and chicken factories,
                            thick-boned and deplumed,
                sacred plumes of gagging monoxides
                                    eclipsing azure,
        Elephant Heart Plums, sacred,
                    compost, compote, cotton gnats, sacred too,
                    guns plunged through car windows,
                            the windows,
                                shards of color,
                        street lamps in all directions, sacred,
        Impalas dragging tail
                in metallic flake saffron
                            airbrush burn Popocatépetl
                                    rebozo flowing lava
                                            sacred,
        trailer parks and horseshoes,
                    spent condoms, the blood on the carpet,
            bottle caps hammered on trunks of trees,
                    abandoned carousels,
                        stereos pulsing in the throat,
        sacred.

*

The second death:
          Came from a tower of papier-mâché
          amidst the sneering eyes of the projects
                    and frigid TV dinners,
barren bus stops and unemployment lines,
               a phalanx of reapers armed with golden shields
               issued by the public in ballot boxes
                         and rigged elections,
        a nickel-plated bullet piercing
               drab doorways into half-dead hearts of men
     —only considered men on tax returns and obituary
     columns,
                    and by the women who swill beer at their
                                             expense,
     and then a wristwatch heirloom from an old man to his
     grandson,
               desert turquoise in the eyes of molded silver,
                    South Texas gypsy campesino,
          a halo of breath escaping the body,
     and then a chair weaver
        from the mountains of Nuevo Léon,
               painter of strange lotteries,
                    a devil's tender spear, stairwells leading
                    nowhere—
     who I once saw suck
        the god end
     of a cactus spike
        and hallucinate Yeshua
     rainbows above the highway
        where deadly manures stir
               in the pearl center of table grapes
                    tucked in a cove along the bountiful foot
                         of the Sierra Nevadas—

Erasmo!
   I say your name and hear the clarion wails
      of a thousand egrets lofted in the willows like upturned
                                    tears waiting to drop
Erasmo, where are your chairs now?
        In what cave do you find yourself, sulking acrylic
   abstractions in the dark?
Erasmo—who sleeps in the melancholic sag of a hammock and
                                      waits

      for the company of an abandoned accordion
          smashing Mexican pulp
              in the blinding guajillo seed
                      of sunrise.

  *

      Saint Gabriel;
      B-ball dreamer,
      lost in rural tendril of vine and barbed wire and late night
                                taco truck
                          philosophies.
What of buche?
        How it glistens vulnerable with the sensuality of a
                            tender throat.
How the lengua?
        Offering hymns to congregations with deaf ears.
Why tripas?
        Mad holy cow with incest in the skull,
      we celebrate your return with sacrifices and pyres
      smoldering in the stomachs
      of empty tin drums
      somewhere in the hearts
      of narrow towns tucked

amidst tilled soil and track houses
and the vanishing plots of empty dirt
where man has yet to break ground.
San Gabriel;
patron saint of discarded dreams,
here the cry of new voices suffering
in methamphetamine fields,
where crouch the stillborn
harvesting stoned crutches
and bleeding karmic livers
that run and pollute the unearthed mineral of drink.

Valley of strip malls and manure,
glittering drags of cocaine and hydraulic chariots
who creep the dusk trail of moons & onyx pathways,
where Friday night drive-throughs and panting liquor
stores
hustle north face with the same evangelical promise
of prescribed medicines
that jolt the South Side Wives Club
into misshaped injections and unnatural jawlines
—noses in the china cabinet!
San Joaquin Valley,
where tired faces water quaint gardens with cut hoses,
bending to bury
the corn next to the sugarcane, reaching
for the avocado on the highest branch,
the melon's elusive fragrance
in all directions toward all the windows in all the houses on all
the streets,
sweet invisible nectars   drifting
in vastness of big sky
where taunts a   kite

                              broken   free

        of its

                                                        strings.

        *

                St. Jack
of the holy waters,
                why have you split your aqueducts
like you split your lover's legs,
                and chastity cemented her fertile ravines?
And now the trout aspire for wings
                and each day awaken with the lust to fly
                among the swallowtails and catapult Devil's Ridge
fluttering gills among the white majesty of solar fans
                down into the peninsula,
                where fled generations before generations
that returned defeated and aged,
                gambling their luck on offspring
                        and dueling religions.

        *

        I sing the praises of the campos,
                the pale trains and panaderos baking sweet bread
                        before Venus's bashful face vanishes in the fold of
                                                                night,
and the worker vans hum engines and stutter into sunrise,
                the campos where dirty faced infants
                crawl among swept gravel and jump rope
                        escapularios blessed in DDT showers,

campos like poorly sewn seams on the ragged end of
a skirt
flittering on invisible zephyrs
living prophetic corridos
on the nylon strings of a splintering vihuela,
campos in the ghostly architecture of dissolved Chinatowns
across the tracks   from the sports arena,
where line the glistening gutters with erect meters and
expiring clocks,
where behind the Kearny Fish Market jezebels cop
nasty paychecks
& spend the day drunk on dumpster juices,
campos of Ararat, where stirs the inconsolable gait of the
Avenger's eyes
lurking among the poppies, gun smoke unfurling
loose fogs of Yettem,
and the campos of Oaxaca
who speak wrecked dialects of Mixtec,
pawing piña against a wail of dueling tubas,
and the campos of Portugal and
Cambodia,
hovels of corn stalk and bamboo—

Internment everywhere!
Internment in the cherry blossoms and whispering
magnolia—
Internments of jade and alabaster drowned in silk—
Internments on Houston & N.E. 4th Street,
where mohawkcholadykes ball gangbangers
initiated under Belmont Street black lights,
and down-low councilmen
bask in golden showers, bugling bull elk speak
to the hustling gargoyles of ghetto zoos—

Chukchansi internments!
Mono chump change rattling powwow horse prayers
at the methadone clinic—
Internments of aborted fetuses and undocumented
brassieres
pinned to clotheslines
wavering for a breast—
Middle-class interning students with immigrant tongues
and five fingered candles
lit 'round the clock—
Yokohama blurring Oklahoma dust,
calligraphic internments scrawled
with brass heron beak & feathers of mud,
unmarked codices translate the demolition,
Laos and the Philippines
—elsewhere.

*

San Joaquin—
where sickly bodies of old Texan mothers draped in aprons
of sunflower
and waning seasons sit idly by, waiting for some slick cancer
to escort
their last days to proms of disintegration, while the souls
of amputated limbs
twitch anxious habits for work loads of the waiting day,
and the cemeteries crowned in tornado fences, warped
from the weight
of age, keep porch poets and lesser known names,
scrawled in Krylon
hieroglyph over barbed boughs and broken pipes,
cemeteries huddled
in shadows of obese mortar castles that have impregnated the

land with palm trees,
where no such trees exist.

*

San Joaquin Valley, why are your back roads stricken
with altars,
and your plastic carnations entombed among deflated
balloons?
What keeps the tattered photographs from disintegrating
with the dew?
Who dies in the back of a narrow van,
limbs splayed to the heavens?
Who survives?
Who arrives first?
Who will harvest the bodies?
Who'll recall them in a dream?
How does one return the belongings?
When names fade where do they go?
What country will claim the purgatoried?
What is the geography of hell?
Who inherits the wreckage?
How deep the ravine of a child's memory?
Are there two sides to the swallowtail's account?
What business has the worm entering the
persimmon?
What galaxies in the mollusk?
Whose bell in the pelvis?
Do crucifixes exclude?
What irrigation of blood?
Does a fig weep in the open air?
Does water discriminate?

What of sirens?
How do we count the invisible?
Can angels scale border walls?
Who will open the gates for them?
Who denies them?
What manner of love is this?

NATURAL TAKEOVER OF SMALL THINGS

How can I tell you that I know nothing
about migrations, though there are pieces of me
left in the chamber of a Glock 35
from back in the day, when I adhered
to the mystical uncertainty of gutters?

How can I tell you that I have worked no land
but the copious things I've grown unintentionally;
like facial hair, or morning breath, or one more
habit I will grow old with?

How can I tell you that when I first bit into a Fuyu
persimmon, dusk tasted this way, the afternoon
my grandfather died—a thick wedge of air, sweetened
by an emptiness?

The more I tell you I am not, the more I am convinced
that the eyespot of a peacock's plume stares, knowing
it will later in the right hands become the object
of some misspent lust, or a tassel on the rearview mirror
of an abandoned Chevy pickup truck on the outskirts,
surrendering its wheels to sediment, bequeathing its engine
to the natural takeover of small things.

INSTRUCTIONS FOR THE ALTAR

Once I have slipped from my skin into sediment
amidst salted alluvials
gathering east of the Rockies
or among the sagging algodón
defeated by valley fog
in preparing the altar
follow these instructions:

I have no regrets
therefore no water is necessary
for dim ablutions,
rather, let the dirtiness of smoke
recall the unpredictability of my name

When I awoke, I did so knowingly
I have never been afraid of the dark,
yet, when I shut my eyes
the invisible becomes apparent

There are no heavens where heavens await,
    no pyramid but in the sternum,
only angels and corrupt deities now;

Release the sage from its bundle,
    the scapulary too

Release the tooth of a snowflake
   from its own sudden drift

To what water does the arroyo submit?

Release the gnarled bough in holy books

Release this name
and all that it conjures;
not the kiss or penetration,
not the naïve boy whistling by the ditch bank
somewhere on an obscure hillside,
or the father's tenderness
moment after moment;

I see you standing against
the dull saffron of a Western sun
and think of how one enters the world headlong,
devoted to the flesh,
born majestic,
bloodied & writhing,
no mind prayers concocted—

      origin of prayer
      someplace else

            origin of plum blossom
            one beat before the scent

   origin of suffering
   various hells occur simultaneously

origin of Juan Diego
a fruit stand south of Delano

origin of Nirvana
ass flat burnt from too much now

origin of the Kingdom
tenderness of the heart

origin of Samsara
consistently returning

origin de Fé
si Diosito quiere

origin of Ahimsa
a teardrop tattoo

origin of Allah
prostration of kisses

origin of Olé
Allah caught in the act

If after these preparations
I still have yet to return
then do as we discussed
that one slow night over a six pack
& bagful of spent pistachio seeds,
about how you wouldn't search for me
  in lush blue cemeteries,

about how you wouldn't pray for me
   at magnolia shrines every Day of the Dead,
about the emptiness of an altar
   and the tiny flickering candle
   above the golden chalice
   that rests atop your collarbone,
instead, make offerings to the blessed
   calling of impermanent gut
   —move on.

FLYING PARALLEL

While driving home from work this evening
a hawk flew parallel to my window.
In its talons a baby squirrel tousled,
its wide black eyes alert to its situation
as the ground fell beneath.

Another bird, smaller in size,
came to the squirrel's rescue, pecking the head
and back of the hawk, parallel to my window.

The squirrel's tail spun, as if a disengaged
propeller ascending between two cliffs.
On one side the crags of sure death.
On the other, a small glimpse of what it
means to be reborn.

Parallel to my window, there were three lives
midflight, each of them arguing about their differences.
None of them prepared to let go.

MY NAME IS HERNANDEZ

After Martin Espada

It means descendent of Hernán Cortés.

Said, Spaniard who slayed Moctezuma
        and a nation of ore,
occupied territories

known since as Southwest. Enslaved captives
        who stewed in marshes of mud and thicket,
forced to shoulder slabs of obsidian,

tear tule from root, to shape

        indestructible pylons of new empire rising—

Though I am not this dramatic by any means.
        I watch television in my boxer shorts,
eat sardines from the can, breath on my children's faces

just to watch them shriek.

My name is Hernandez.
        My father is a field worker. Every sugar beet
you've ever eaten he's shorn away what threatened to destroy it.

When I was born he wore me on his back
           while slouching over a short-handled hoe
in the monsoon plains of five Wyoming summers.

There is too much time for memory to be accurate.
              My father's worked since the day of his conception.
A shoeshine boy in the parlors of south Texas.

              The adobe tiles were relics
from days of indentured servitude. Earthen red clay shingles
           the boy destroyed with rifle.

              Mesquite is what he recalls mostly.
And how the chicharra's song is a quantum thread between
                                                          this life

and that. I see him now, behind the wheel of a rig,
              hazardous materials, head a snowcapped
slab of insidious worry. Illuminated by the coo

of a grandson,
              the most fragile ammonite coiled in the shape
of his own quavering hand.

              My name is Hernandez.
Born of a woman who was born of a woman…
              though I've said this once before.
Don't let her flexible disposition fool you. Consider the blade
                                            of a palm leaf,

on Palm Sunday.
Consider the Sabbath, Ash Wednesday.
          She is devoted to the countdown
of years, starting from ten. Her time here is limited.
          Same is true for the rest of us.
Except she has gotten good at forgetting this.
          We haven't.
We miss. She lets on a permanence, not seen since
          the resurrection.

My name is Hernandez.
Of a Dinuba Sanitarium that crumbled in '89.

Of an elementary school hidden between a plum orchard
          and the voluptuous golden thigh of a foothill.
Of an education that included the neon powder of sulfur.

Of menial jobs—fast-food dives and an auto detailing stint.
          Of thirty days in the Tulare County Jail,
and then five more.

Of flea markets and strip malls.
          Of television 'round the clock.
Of relationships to things and people that rarely go the distance.

Of the punk rock eighties and pierced orifices.
          Of the Dionysian Festival in the vagabond
Corfu forest of '92.

Of constantly risking solitude.
　　　　Of the grandfather on Magnolia Way,
who pickles eggs in a tin shed behind a sulking house with two
　　　　　　　　　　　　　　　　　　　mortgages.

Of the twin abortions.
　　　　Of regrets.
Of saying things like regret because it's expected.

Of reneging on words.
　　　　Of doctoring the wounds with words.
Of admitting he knows nothing of words.

Years ago, while living in South San Francisco, I walked into a
　　　　　　　　　　　　　　　　　　　carniceria
　　　　with my last name emblazoned on the window.
A young man draped in a blood apron greeted me.

I ordered three tacos de lengua, and smiling
　　　　I told him that I was a Hernandez too.
Yes, he replied.

Handing me the change.
　　　　Dicing the cow's last word on the cutting block, he said,

There are millions of us here.

Millions of Hernandezes.
　　　　Each one
expecting some kind of deal.

ADIOS, FRESNO

You could use more letters of love.
      Here, take these. You owe me nothing, except back pay.
   But I won't mention it again.
        Trust me when I say I'll have no regrets leaving you.
   Sure, I'll hear it from the homebodies
        and deadpan hearts, who were born, loathe,
           and beg to die
              amid the drugged poppies.

You can keep your fields; the sun will follow me.

      I won't reconsider.
        I've overstayed my welcome
          by three generations.

The musicians will be alright
   by which I mean incomparable,
      by which I mean they get the work done.
   A G-string hangs over the baseball stadium on opening
                         night
      when the whores go two-for-a-buck
   beneath the peeling paint of home-run alley.

        Fresno, your mosques are waning
      and your restaurant kitchens are wetter
          than before.

Even the hungry are gutting cows in the pasture now.

The farmers buy their vegetables in supermarkets, you know?

There is a difference between lost and Laos.

One day you will have all the water you need.

The statue of David of Sassoon could use a rest, Fresno.

Don't bother looking for me.
    I will be lost to myself for the next hundred cycles,
        on a mountain near Red Feather Lakes.
    Caught up in raising three children who won't
                      mistake
            the humming of bees
        for their own ambition.

Fresno, I can see your underwear through the holes in your jeans.

        If I wanted to be politically correct I would
                      have
        registered my vehicle.

I won't miss the pretense,
    or the way your midnight reeks of pissed yeast and salami.
    I might miss the smell of a huele de noche during baseball
                      season.
        Or the cut grass at Shahzade Field.
            —damn, you're playing to my nostalgia
                      again.
    It's all you're good for.

I'm glad you and I never had children.
There would've been this thing of blood between us.
                              Don't get sappy on me.

    Outside the truckers are grinding their axles,
        and the exhaust pipes got the bulldogs going next door.

You look pitiful when you're in love.
                              I didn't say beautiful.
This drought suits you.
            Am I being too hard? You'll get over it.
The refrigerator almost burnt down the house
        last night and I kept thinking somehow
            you were responsible for it.

            The bullet hole in my fence can only stare so long.

My cousin Art is in rehab now, but the silos
                        won't shut up.
The landscape talks the loudest shit in summer.

    Fresno, you try too hard.
                Why'd you have to take

                        —Mia Barraza
                        —Andres Montoya
                        —Victor Martinez

                        from us?

Fresno, I might return if you promise to be good.

Just that I can't stand the heat.

There are too many I-can't-stands.

As many fruit stands.

My mind is a packinghouse

with a sagging conveyor belt.

Strawberries should taste so tart.

Oranges should fit in the palm of an adult
hand.

There's no such thing as windfall.

A pluot is incest at its finest.

Enough said, Fresno.   Adios.

CULTURE OF FLOW

. . . don't put your finger out, don't dare put your finger out,
because the pigeons are eating meat now,
because the baby calf, fed on milk, and kept tender
in total darkness, is buying a gun.
Inside books the trees are screaming revenge.

—Victor Martinez, *National Geographic*

CULTURE OF FLOW

Propaganda

        tsunamis the tilted metropolis

                (ashe Fukushima—

E V E R Y
      W H E R E

    wind

water

               torrent

   welfare
      wars of water
       wind down
  from Sierra Nevadas
or the great Colorado nimbus dream
      Where Water Flows Food Grows
     read the billboards of the backroads
     and the highways—
  Dust devils spin words,
 the illusory image
   of water glances

a blow across the Big Bank Vault
water so fluid, becomes politico form
                    the sand dollar
                              drops
            in New Orleans
    Haiti   Lost
                              Lake

        where Hmong,
                Mexicanos, Mixtecos & other

immigrantalienwetbackrefugees

            remix a song from the pages of Popol Vuh,
              —limp poles fish for suckers
                    and empty cans bob, hands bend and dig
            the earth, the betabel, red as graffiti tag
                        sprayed in Yokut grinding hole,
    no body of water draws lines so

            no bank so rigid
            to bend the currency
                or force the point of
                        liquidity)
                    fluid
            flush

Fish or man?

Them or us?

                Big water takes little water.

(as in the fable
of Narciso who
        discovered
a formlessness that had already been
        discovered
before any thought
  of discovery
  had been patented by Cortés
                —Slayer of Seven Waters.

{ EROSION }

        At the end of the day—
what do I know about flow
      or flood?
Or how an ammonite
affects a mountain peak
        authored by the cherub plume
of the Creator's handless hand
and mindless mind?
What do I really know
of the acequia, or the evergreen,
        or of Muir's nagging limp, for that
                  matter,
What about switchbacks?
Who really knows the depths of the Brewer Bird's black?

(True account #1:
I once saw sunlight
spill from a Walking Weed
pressed between pages
of John Muir's journals—
    in the stem was the same luminosity
        that happens each spring
            when the sun cuts through
                the bullshit
      of all Great Valleys.

{ WEIR }

(True account #2:
For years I'd only known
    John Muir as a wooden bust
  carved in an obscure tree trunk
    that sits on Highway 99
  near the Greyhound bus station   on the outskirts of
                  Goshen, California

(where homeboys drift in 40 oz. sedentary oceans—
    (where soft-eyed campesino children
catch the long bus-ride back to Linnell Camp,
    pointing out the bearded Muir, whose nose sits sun-
                  bleached
      beneath a perfectly clear
      brown
      sky.

{ RAINDROPS }

The front page news is
Linnell Camp on a bad day,
otherwise nameless.

.

Even in Linnell,
            how I long to taste Linnell
                        in the darkest plum.

.

On the truck bed, two
young girls giggle, while dreaming
beyond el campo.

{ DAM }

Avocado Lake—
            miniature cobalt mire
                        flooded raza tributary
Caló rhythms in the sand
            scent of grilled meat,
                        downstream cut off
                        shorts/ half shirts/ ice chests
            & frozen weenies
                        tube tops sticky in gravy heat
            all exposed—
tooth of breast

slug of crotch
        clam of ass
    slime of soles
a cross-pollination of tongues and fluids
            all detritus of the people
                scattered like Hell Notes—

Avocado Lake
            where unlike indocumentados
    muskrats can scurry
        in and out
                of wetness—

Avocado Lake
        tundra of Mennos
    downstream the cemetery
        the white columns   concrete markers
                & wavering flags sullen   in dead heat
                    unsavory froth of silt
                    & overspray
                downstream
            the invisible
        campos of Agraria—overspray on
    flannel of withering Dinuba,
on Orosi's gray poppies, out to where
            Yettem sows nostalgia
                of Ararat,
to where Madera ossifies into Oaxaca,
                    overspray on Pinedale (1942
            where five thousand hyphenated
                eyes got interned
                —impulse panacea

broke Nikkei

like levies.

{ AGUA BENDITA }

Sunday
service begins,
pews do as they do
knelt idled like old logs
bent behind the other
eiderdown book jackets
held between saintly nail-
beds with rotted moons
from grease work of
two months night-
shift succulents
go weeks
without
water
+
crosses
are for boring
plows pew strips
of brown
golden green-
stalk erect-
ions of prayer
filtering through
light from glass atrium

Spanish service is always held
at noon or midnight
where day spik in tongues
absolute grapes and great hosts
ration like embers
or a gang of flies
gorging on
an open
-ing

*

God is the habit.

Agraria the whore.

The trinity exists.

Only where you plant it.

Confession happens at sunrise.

The Padre dispenses.

Windfall wafers.

Baptisms will happen without.

Interim flows.

Drought gone to quails.

Maize gasoline martyrs.

Blues fissure-man sucking.

Siphon staff clean of fossil & sediment.

Weirs crack brujeria curses.

Still the seepage lolls on.

Aqueduct turn water tables turn.

Almond root gives way to.

Channel number five.

Perfumes horizon zygote.

Rouge skyline methamphetamine.

Silos elected in grove chambers and secret compartments.

Tule is only half the name.

Slough sounds like this for a reason.

Terminator seed does just that.

Dam.

(Hydration
of hydrous asteroid,
    the Kuiper belt out past
Neptune, the Oort cloud on the edge
        primitive members
of our universe gather   frozen fossils
    long past epoch   rock and metal
      Water of four billion years   a bombardment of systems
                    lunar   cataclysm
                wasn't until the moon became   pock-marked,
                    the earth was able to retain more
                because it retained less
                    of itself through meteoric assault—
                        the more   holes
                                in the body
                the more capacity   for water
        the   more   impressionable
    the planet
                        the more   the more water
whereas the moon   lost
                                its water
            to the absence of gravity—

                but retained
                    its integrity
                during the debate.

{ DITCH }

Proof is in the detritus—
      a night magpie
    squirming on a bough,
      a phantom squirrel slavering
   headlong in the dumpster
        cherry pits
       & swollen diapers,
     warped heaps of newspaper,
coffee grounds smear out
     clusters of flies bickering
        maggot wars reveal
          headlines of faded ink
    about an uprising in a Oaxacan schoolyard
     a battalion of broken pencils
    marched off paper
       onto dirt roads
      fingers abandoned desk-side
  scrawling aloud in the Zócalo
    about the inadequacies of lead
        while apple cores suffocate
   beneath ribs of broken cabinet
& rancid meat
     decomposing in stink of starlight
        that offers reason enough
    for a fog.

{ FOG }

In the campos of central California
      it is said that the tule fog
          is the wandering spirit
      of Tiburcio Vásquez & his men
      (the martyred guerrilla
whose family was massacred   in the rush of 1849—
    this contradicts the tule's humble nature,
    tule from tullin,
          Nahuatl for *gentle thorn*
    of which Tenochtitlan is built upon
      there are tule canoes of Yokut,
        there is Tule Lake,
      internment camps of World War II
            Tulares marsh of Tullin
    Tulares of exiled Dragons
      & whispering methane
        & John Deere carcasses
    strewn along the aqueduct
  forgotten and corrugated
half buried antler plows, skull of jackrabbit
        with one ear flittering in brown breeze,
    all detritus melds to sediment eventually,
        time will erode the hardest of us,
while somewhere   lost along the Kaweah shore,
    a single soda bottle is sneaking
        wet kisses   in a thistle's ear.

{ IRRIGATION }

The foothills roil the heels
        beneath small bridges
and venous aqueducts
      spiced with atrazine,
         where spiders wolf the rosemary,
   where egret and wren
            dumb-sex the other in marshlands,
with tufts of tule, silhouettes of awkward gothic
    factories encroach
          and gag airborne corrosion
          (rust is the color
                of wheat at three sixteen
     in the afternoon   (in early November
        in the Year of Methane
      palm fronds felled by the tracks
  dissolve to exoskeletons kneeling
      for a Dia de los Niños Santos
   ritual sipping up spewed
     trickle of irrigation
        from loins of the reservoir
shadowing the gutting factory
        beneath old Uranus
    where the stink of offal
warms its way through
           the neighborhoods, crippled
  by the music
      of incestuous cattle screwing

  —or some other curse,
      born from a book,

professed in the desperate
grooves of sudden drought,
        mistook for something that sounded
like an answer.

{ GUTTER }

(Witnessing the situation, the mayfly, of
course said nothing, its lips were sealed, its
only purpose, to seek out female and
impregnate, write a check monthly to cover
the expenses, and pray its offspring would
not, years later, come seeking a past,
dependent on rumor.

HOW TO GET TO THE SAN JOAQUIN RIVER

To get to the river
         you must first answer
to Lawson Inada
            at a Lost Lake tollbooth.

 He might offer an enigma
             or direct you to Pinedale—
a once internment camp, but now mostly
            pit bulls and Chevy carcasses
           have the run of it,
     where on Sunday mornings
             you'll find Raoul "El Charro" Hernandez
             bellowing *Cielito Lindo*
          clad in suit of lights
     while drowning hangover
            in bloody tripe.

To get to the San Joaquin River
             you have to get back in your car
     and head the other way
toward Friant Dam,
     or the city of Xibalba,
toward your grandmother's ashy knuckles,
        and then walk
     two hundred and thirty miles
            from Sunrise Market to the State Capitol
     where everything is about water.

To get to the San Joaquin River
             you have to find Orosi bluesman,
                  Lance Canales
       and he will sing to you that, *San Joaquin River*

    is Choinumne slang
         meaning burial ground
       for irrigation heyday
            gone awry—

                    is Hoinumne folk phrase,
                         meaning build it or lose it—

    is Mono battle cry
       meaning us or the fish—
            is Tachi prayer to mend
                broken bird wings
                     torn blankets
                  and fear—

is Chukchansi parable
    for the sparkling strip
       that numbs the people
         from themselves—

                     is Yokut poem
                  expressing the beginning
                     of the end—

To get to the San Joaquin River
             you'll have to make a U-turn
       at Old Mesilla, or El Paso
       or a left at Oaxaca's Guelaguetza,

drive about fifteen city blocks
—if you reach Quezón City
you've gone too far,
get back in your car
and look for Ester Hernandez's *Sun Mad* billboard
on Highway 99.

To get to the San Joaquin River,
you have to enter
the WIC office on Blackstone Avenue,
forget about dying your roots,
buy an electric wheelchair instead,
own a child
with his mother's last name,
but don't park in the loading zone,
because the pawn shop closes early
and the standing guitars
can only wait for so long.
Whatever you do,
don't subscribe to the brotherhood
that measures their worth in shoes,
or Roman numerals,
or words,
or how many home runs a man can catch
while standing
in the alley of wasted dreams.

SKIN TAX

My story gets told in various ways:
a romance, a dirty joke, a war, a vacancy.

—Rumi

To touch my person to someone else,
is about as much as I can stand.

—Walt Whitman

MAMA'S BOY

They say I'm a Mama's Boy
    like it's a bad thing, when all along
        I thought that's what a man was.
They say my skin was made from goat's milk
      & dandelions
        and that my eyes were plucked
            from cherry blossom in the month of February

A Mama's Boy they say,
    with hands too soft for picking
    legs thin as sprigs of mesquite
      They say my voice lacks
          the asphalt grit of courage, that I
          should work on it
            and that my name is too short
               to call me by name,
                  and they're right

When they say
    I was born with a hole in my heart
    the size of a tiny fish eye. They're right
        when they shout Mama's Boy
          and poke at the tenderness that is my back
      claiming that my hair was quilted from a beggar's scarf
        and that my smile was strewn from tender husks of
                        sugarcane
        it's true—

Since I've fondled and groped at the inside
    of my mama's womb,
        just a squirming confirmation of father's lust,
      I've scheming ways to retreat to that
        warm familiar sack of membrane
            and love manifold

This is why
I lead with the docile nose of a house cat
    speak my intentions
      in raw doggerel utterances
from the stiff core of a loose core of a taciturn tongue
      Why I tweeze the nose hair clean
        behind locked doors
    using the reflection off surgical steel buck-knives
        & limp toilet handles
          lather my jaw with baking powder and lava rock
          skin tax
          for the morning peel
        Because I am soft,
          zephyr soft
        and teeming with secrets

I am the watermark of houses submerged
    My whimpering howl a rivulet of what remains
        from the hidden
      tidal tears of men
        Which is why they do not lie when they say
        my feeble knees are the silken steel edges
      of grandfather's worn plow discs
        tease that my stomach is a sofa cushion

stuffed with the down of a thousand geese
and that my nipples are the fragile embroidery
of Victorian gowns

My words,
they say, these boyish longings,
do not pounce from the gut like

    alloy   drum   fire
      candy   wine   lingo

do not come on like

    razor   neck   nicks
    splashed in allspice   fire

will not crowbar the ribcage
will not shoehorn the chunk boot
or adorn the rearview in

    deer   hoof   rabbit
    knuckle   luck charms

Instead, they are made from
sugar water & pomegranate lust
jelly for the dawn song
warm rhythms for the doubtful eye &
the accusing heart

It is because of this,
they jab their crooked fingers in my face

and shout, *Mama's Boy!*
    like it's a bad thing
   when all along, you see,
                I thought
     that's what a Man was.

I RUB MY HANDS

With your cream
Cocoa butter & aloe
On my skin reminds me of the time
I've denied your love

In the supermarket
When your hand slips into the curve of my back pocket
and you whisper kisses
against the meat of my neck

I pull away—
A man afraid of what message
affection might bring,
What foolishness

if I leaned into you
And took honest love
anytime you wanted it

What foolishness if I nipped back at you
With puckered lips, like an infant
gurgling at the coo of his mother's voice

and a passerby
catches me,
in love,
being lovely with you
and your woman ways

Worse yet, another man
with wife in tow

spots me gurgling
putty dumb

eyes aglow
and walk away thinking thoughts
of how foolish I appear
stripped down by my lover's side
balls braided at the flimsy tips
of thin fingers

How silly I'd appear
cutting loose at the sight of you
'round every corner
in every movie house

Romanced madly
pecking at your affection
like a kitten clucks
at its mother's tit

Love gazed &
Lathered by you
and the hands that lotion themselves
with cocoa butter & aloe

I reject your touch
and love you from where I stand
because stepping closer
would mean leaving this place

I have lived for a lifetime
Have carved from granite, soot, &
dirty skin

I deny myself
of the child I become
when sharing a meal
with you.

spooning
hot soup into one another's open mouth
I peer inside and wonder

If the bed
of my tongue exposed
looks as tender
and vulnerable as yours

If I am a man
then you will not see
the inside of my mouth
taking in anything

by you or your giving spoon
in a crowded space
where a passerby might stare
think me hungry

I deny your love
and pay the price nightly
smother my skin
in cocoa butter & aloe

slide fingers between fingers
drowning calluses
hand over hand
touching, whiffing deeply

like a puppy burrowing
into an inviting crotch
gobbling at the warm scent
of living

remembering the times
I've denied myself publicly
of your affection
for fear of a passerby

spotting me in love
being lovely
with you
and your woman ways.

I ARRIVE LATE

You are on your back
wrapped in a paper gown

your clothes lie limp
in bundles beside you

your toenails are chipped
and ridged like candy apples

in the white white
loneliness of waiting

you remain still,
shining like a nickel

tucked beneath the icebox.
I search for your face

hidden beneath the mass of forearm
and thick tassels of your hair

a gauze panty doused in blood sticks
to the cold linoleum floor and

tears have fallen everywhere.
I want to cradle you

place your head in my lap and strum
the tufts of wet strands

away from your mouth, but I am afraid
affection is what brought us here.

Your hand reaches out and lifts
a sad finger pointing

down beneath my seat
where you placed a small plastic cup

for me to consider.
I lean over to look and must focus my eyes:

a violet wad
of bulbous flesh.

This, you say, *is my fault,*
my body hates me.

I want to speak but breath has abandoned me.
The smell of latex unfurls over the silence

until both become unbearable.
In a bolt of heat my stomach contracts

to hold itself,
causing the hair on my arm to lift

as if in defiance
of my own skin.

I PISSED ON LITTLE RICKY

because the guys dared me to.
 He was in a sandbox hunched over

plowing his Tonka truck through tiny dunes when
 Pelón, his big brother, left him there to get more toys.

I had to go pee real bad, and one of the guys blurted
 I dare you to piss on him! So I did,

impulsively spraying on his powder brown hair.
 A fiery gush of yellow went stinging down his face,

drowning his soft shoulders, scalding his little eyes,
 and we ran.

Behind us, his tiny lungs exhausted
 every bit of air they held

out into the vacant valley sky
 —and we laughed.

Days later, while at school, a crop duster blew past our playground,
 its overspray stung my face like a hornet's dagger,

unraveling a ribbon of blood that clung
 from my nose and wrapped around me,

ending in a fancy knot.

PERCHED ON THE FACE

For my grandmother, Estela Constante

    of a moon in a 1949 photograph
is how you'll exist in this poem.
The faded image of your tight blouse and

bobby socks glee framed in billowing tendrils

    black as licorice
did no favors for your heart. It wasn't that the radio
dedicated slow songs to young lovers split by war,
or that the man you romanced called a flat bed pickup

    home.
Not even the sweetness of your cherry lip gloss
could save you from the tired gray of this photo,
much less from the worn back of the field hand's fate.

    It wasn't that South Texas
hated your skin and called you a Greaser because
your hands. By age ten were thick enough to withstand
the sting of a ruler, and dark enough to

    neglect the bruises.
It wasn't because he promised you lush acreage
tucked amidst infinite landscapes, solid workloads,
and sunsets, with brilliant stars to silhouette
the dreams,

that made peculiar nights seem less
of an affair than his mustache would conceal.
Not even when you delicately brushed your lashes in
long strokes, pinched your cheeks to a warm fluster,
and dabbed rosemary on the bed of your wrists, did
you discover a breath to call your own.

It was when the photographer flirted,
focused his lens, gently draped a black cloth over his eyes,
then asked you to smile—and you never stopped.

IF I COULD TELL YOU

about the loss
    I've suffered in the bearing
month of May

   About the orchid blown
from its supple root or
    how the calla lily cracked its bell

then you would see clearly
    that death and a cherry blossom
   are of the same seed

  And that a garden smiles
with the brilliant teeth of hunger
    and that my sadness isn't sadness at all

but a prayer for the passing
    a peach blossom to a peach
      a fallen plum

   bursting crimson from the bruised skin
of its cheek
    a cactus flower leaning

  against the joy of daybreak
And maybe then you would not forget
    that somewhere in the glorious

luster of birth
there are petals opening
to close as if by magic

And if you did not catch them
if you did not bury your nose against their belly
then you will not hear

how they are mapping out
your body when it rests
when it touches ground

again.

ENTER MADRUGADA

with loose pants and leather sandals
a wide-brimmed hat with a black band

and lipstick on your deep cherry guayabera.
You staggered with a swagger into morning

remembering all the lines you fed the sequin-clad mujer
of yesterday's tardeada, who you flirted with and tried

to kiss until she laughed at you because she knew you
had a wife, six kids, a garden, and
an empty doghouse.

So you requested a song by Little Joe hoping he could take you
back to Tejas and all of this would be a drunken hallucination.

When the accordion kicked in you jerked your hips like a
                                                    teenager
at prom, trying to impress all the viejas with your timeless
                                                    rhythm

but it didn't work—at first.
As the night crept you insisted on gambling your paycheck

and bought margaritas for every woman that approached
                                                    the bar,
hoping it would be enough to fire up conversation,

until finally it was. Her name—well, you forgot after
the introduction, but it didn't matter because she spoke to you

like a true Tejana and that was enough reason to slow dance
the night away. When your zipper burned,

she knew what this would come down to, you both did.
After all the touching and breathing and moving in sync

After all the heat and sweat and exhaustion
After all the liquor and adrenaline, and your maleness,
                            and her femininity

After all the lights expired and music retired,
the only thing left for chance was that small
        Thanks-for-everything kiss on the neck, which you
kindly accepted.

Enter madrugada.
        Enter with nopales, tomate, cebolloa y chile
        Enter with familia, a wife, a garden, and an empty doghouse

dreams of Tejas and a loose wallet,
now enter with lipstick on your deep cherry
                                    guayabera.

I'M GOING TO PUT VIRGIL DOWN

If you are a poet, then you will see clearly that there
is a cloud floating in this sheet of paper.
—Thich Nhat Hanh

right here on this cloud
   in front of you
  so that you can't mistake him
   for another brother

with his mama's curls
  sloven in iguana skin belt
alacran güero
    in the buckle,

   a white stinger for protection.
I'm gonna howl
  against the emptiness of this page
so that you don't mistake the monsoon

   of his black luck for
another lowlife passing in the night

Listen—
   Hear the man clank hammers?
     Listen to his *heave ho!*
Hear it?
     This is Virgil
     Leather-necked foreman of American hoods
     King of the desert

Of wrought iron &
    crumbling highways
Of enchanted lands &
      poisonous addictions

This is how he dances
  when he is right—
    el gusano
      the drunken worm of agave

When he is wrong
    the dance is visceral
      his guts rumble, the heart plucks the ribcage
    a throbbing liver keeps tempo

Look—
    You can see black musical notes
   slipping from the scars
      a sonata of lonesome odes fluttering
  about the fists
   tattoos bouncing from the skin
a birthmark hangs on
    at the temple

This is Virgil
    Father of prison guards &
  missing children
    A mustache of stars
guards the stiffened lip of his jaw
  where secrets are locked
      and romance tumbles

For the woman who kept him—
　　there were greased engines,
　　　rigged pipes,
　　　polaroids,
　　　postcards of saints,
　　　and prayers

In the glove compartment
　　letters of love
　　　　　　& promises
A nicked ring
A dollar bill ripped in two
A million unlabeled keys
　　　　　　& somewhere
a million doors waiting to be opened.

This is Virgil
　in a box
　feeding himself to the earth

El gusano
gobbled by a raven
that swoops from a cornhusk
watered by this cloud
I'm putting him down on,
so that you mistake him
for another brother
　　　in a poem.

WHEN YOUNG ANDRES

For Maceo Montoya, Malaquias & Leslie, and for Daniel Chacon

died before his book came out
not a poet in town could find the words.
Tongues hung

out like crippled raisins,
out like burning flags,
   gagging tears of ash

fire and smoke
weeping smudge stacks in big sky black
holding hands

in the cavity of church
where we gathered for the juice
like fire ants on a gutted grape.

   His voice tilling
tender and desperate at every reading,
praying poets find pulp in poems

when he sang, when he loved,
when he cried out to *GOD!*
      in the University Pit

books clapped shut
ravens jutted from tree limbs
      and rooftops

eyes yanked from lovers' gaits
    students snapped pencils
smeared ink, blinked, and listened.

    In fertile soil,
amid bone orchards, blood dust,
and sweat, where crows clamor and swarm

up in clouds,
where summer ghosts rise from asphalt
    off the 99—

I imagine your voice Andres,
    in the warm baritone of earth,
reciting ice-worker hymns
to seedlings not yet touching sky
lulling the roots of trees, peaches, plums and figs
that will one day ripen to a plump sweetness

nourishing this hunger—
The fruit of our lives
                as you've known it.

ACKNOWLEDGMENTS

Endless gratitude to the following people for their contributions to many of these poems over the years: my parents, Felix and Lydia Hernandez; my benevolent literary familia Juan Felipe Herrera and Margarita Luna Robles; and my brother Jason McDonald. Gratitude to Naropa University for early guidance, especially Jack Collom (RIP), Reed Bye, Junior Burke, Anne Waldman, Keith Abbott (RIP), Indira Ganesan, and Andrew Wille, and to the Bennington Writing Seminars, especially Major Jackson, Amy Gerstler, Timothy Liu, and Ed Ochester. Also, deep bow to my students and colleagues at the University of Texas El Paso Department of Creative Writing for having my back. Love to my inner circle: Ana Saldaña, for being my ray of light in the darkest of times; Estela and Cory Sue; Norma Gonzalez; Felix Duarte; David Herrera; Tony Delfino; Eliseo Carrera; and Larissa M. Gómez Vásquez. Love and gratitude to my extended familia: Daniel Chacon, Mayela Padilla, Alessandra Narvaez Varela, Luis Humberto Valadez, Jennifer Heath, Daniel Grandbois, Kimberly Castillo, Ernesto Mendoza, Nico Cooper, Benjamin Alire Saenz, Seema Reza, Anthony Cody, Bill Clark at Literarity Bookstore, and Tejal Patel. A deep bow of respect and love to the artists, musicians, and poets who have collaborated with me on many performances and experimentations over the past twenty-six years (random order): Alejo Delgado, Carlos

Rodriguez, David Herrera, Jimmy Biala, Raoul J. Hernandez (RIP), Lance Canales, Johnny Irion, Daniel Grandbois, Abelino Bautista, Ted Nunes, Ana Saldaña, Cocó Alcazar, Marissa Rodriguez, Erasmo Garcia, Ramiro Martinez, Ana Suarez, Richard Juarez, Tony Delfino, Mark Silent Bear, Jeremy Hofer, Devoya Mayo, Andrew Treviño, Freddy Saenz, Jonas Berglund, Joel Rafael, David Amram, 40 Watt Hype, Pa' Chango, Aaron Wall, Luis "Squeezebox" Garcia, the Chakra crew, Conjunto Califas, Los Illegals, Adolfo Guzman Lopez, Darren J. De Leon, the Manikrudo fam, Ahimsa Locos, Mezcal, Teatro Zapata, and my early XprMental poetry tribe, Cucuy.

PUBLICATION ACKNOWLEDGMENTS

Selections from *Natural Takeover of Small Things* were written between 2006 and 2012 and published with permission by the University of Arizona Press, Camino del Sol Series, 2013. Selections from *Culture of Flow* were written between 2008 and 2010 and previously published by Monkey Puzzle Press, with special thanks to Nate Jordan. Selections from *Skin Tax* were written between 1996 and 2004 and previously published by Heyday Books, with special thanks to Patricia Wakida and Malcolm Margolin. The line *When I am alone, I am almost enough*, which appears in italics in the poem "Settling," is by the poet Seema Reza. The poem "A Basic Understanding" is taken from a line by Thich Nhat Hanh from his book *The Heart of Understanding*. The line "celebrating itself and singing itself," which appears on page 35, is a reference to the Walt Whitman poem "Song of Myself."

Ana Saldaña

ABOUT THE AUTHOR

Tim Z. Hernandez is an award-winning writer, multidisciplinary artist, storyteller, and research scholar. His work includes poetry, novels, nonfiction, screenplays, and staged productions, and his writing and research have been featured in the *Los Angeles Times*, the *New York Times*, C-SPAN's *Book TV*, and NPR's *All Things Considered*. He is the recipient of numerous awards, including the American Book Award for poetry and the International Latino Book Award for historical fiction, and he was recently recognized by the California State Senate for his work locating the victims of the 1948 plane wreck at Los Gatos, the subject of his nonfiction books that make up *the plane crash series*. Hernandez holds a BA from Naropa University and an MFA from Bennington College. He is an associate professor at the University of Texas El Paso's Bilingual MFA program in creative writing, and he currently lives in El Paso, Texas, with his two children. You can find more info at www.timzhernandez.com.